The Grief Recovery and Beyond

How to Overcome Any Difficulty in Life

Jeff Lawrenson

ISBN Paperback: 978-1-80157-223-1

Printed by IngramSpark

First printing edition 2021.

Table of Content

THE STRENGHT TO GRIEVE

The death of a loved one is the deepest of all sorrows. The sorrow that comes with this loss is deep and multifaceted, impacting our feelings, our bodies, and our lives. Grief is terrifying and depleting. Emotionally, grief is a mixture of raw emotions, such as sadness, anguish, rage, remorse, longing, fear, and deprivation. Grief may be physically perceived as fatigue, emptiness, tension, sleeplessness, or lack of appetite. Grief invades our everyday lives in many unexpected gaps and transitions, such as the empty dining table, or the sudden loss of love and companionship, as well as in many new apprehensions, modifications, and uncertainties. The loss of a loved one brings every part of our lives out of control. The closest we were to the person who died, the more serious the loss is. Love doesn't die easily. It is also mourning to celebrate the depth of the union. Tears, then, are the gems of nostalgia, sad yet glistening with the charm of the past. Then the sadness with its bitterness marks the end ... but it is also the praise of the one who is gone.

In the months of grieving after death, we learn to face the truth and pain of our loss, to say good-bye to the deceased loved one, to restore ourselves and to reinvest in life again. In a way, mourning is a time of fresh mastery

1

over us and our lives. Recovery comes in the days ahead, when mourning is over and a new equilibrium is sought. But until we heal, we have a lot of interactions that will cause our sadness again, before those feelings really dissipate. Finishing or finishing the grieving occurs when we are able to let go of our emotions of grieving and our intense friendship with the deceased. Although our love never dies, the pain of our loss will inevitably dissolve.

While we may feel unaware of grief, grief is, in fact, like a neighbor who still lives next door, no matter where or how we live, no matter how we try to move away. Grief can be the result of any major change or loss of our lives. If we want it or not, any one of us has to learn to let go, to move on without someone or something that we really wanted.

Life is going to change. We are experiencing transition, loss, and grief from birth to birth. Every home venture, every step, every change of job or status, every loss of person, every pet, every belief, every disease, every change of life, such as marriage , divorce, or retirement, and every kind of personal growth and change can be a cause of grief. This is what Elisabeth Kübler-Ross calls the "little dead" of creation. If we had to face everyday changes and practice letting go of our daily lives, then loss and sorrow would be less painful. Even though we have a multitude of chances to learn how to cope with grief, we typically suppress our feelings of loss. We're bearing up and pushing ourselves forward.

Since we deny the full measure of our sadness in our daily adjustments and defeats, when the great sorrows arrive, then the sorrow is new, terrifying, and overwhelming. Nevertheless, the death of a loved one is so great and so final a loss that our past experiences with "little deaths" can never fully prepare us. Most of us have had some experience with good grief. For example, while we often feel alone in our personal grievances, mourners across our nation were encouraged to work together through their grievances when President Kennedy was assassinated. On TV we've seen photos of Kennedy, his life, the circumstances of his death, and his funeral over and over for a few days. We spoke to each other about the loss of the president. We've been reading about his life.

This is the central process of grieving — repeating the photos and emotions of our beloved loved one again and again until the grief process is over. That we can grieve and heal always seems a wonderful accomplishment, but human resilience is incredible. Just like a forest can burn to the ground and eventually rise again, or a city can be destroyed by a flood and rebuilt, so that each one of us can resolve our sorrow, resolve the tremendous loss of our lives, and eventually recover and rebuild our lives. This is the way of nature.

It requires bravery, therefore, to grieve. It takes bravery to experience our pain and face the unknown. It also requires courage to grieve in a society that wrongly values caution, where we risk the exclusion of others by being transparent or different. Open mourners are a select community, able to move through pain and grief and anger to heal and recover. Unfortunately, our myths about grief prevent us from having the courage to confront grief. Many of us fear that, if allowed in, grief would overtake us forever. The reality is that the sorrow endured has vanished. The only grievance that does not stop is the grievance that has not been thoroughly faced.

Grief unexpressed is like a bomb waiting to explode. We misunderstand tears, too. The slang term of crying in our culture is "breaking down." We behave as if weeping is incorrect or akin to disease, while tears actually give us the necessary release of our intense feelings. Another myth is that if we really loved someone, we would never end up with our sadness, as if ongoing sorrow is a testament to our love. But true love does not need sorrow in order to support its reality. Love will last in a happier and more fulfilling way, until our sorrow is dispelled. We should remember our dead better by the quality of our continued lives than by our endless remembrance of the past. Another common misunderstanding is that the pain can not be over.

Finally, there is a common perception that self-denial is part of grief. Healthy sorrow, however, depends on self-care. Self-denial is not a testimony of compassion. Instead, our dead loved one will want us to love ourselves as he or she loved us. How are we going to come to have the strength to grieve? Some of us learn bravery instinctively when we have to act to survive.

Most of us learn the courage to face new challenges in the course of living, witnessing and surviving our hardships over and over. Since pain is inevitable, we should learn to make pain teaching element instead of our enemy. As George Bernard Shaw so aptly put it, "Heartbreak is life educating us." We will learn that raging makes our journey more difficult, exciting and rewarding. One way to practice bravery is to play with being brave. A beautiful example of this was given to me by my friend Peter, who at the age of forty had been told by his doctor that he had lung cancer. Peter was afraid. Then he thought of the woman he loved and how terrified she would be if he gave in to the fear inside himself. As an experiment, he wanted to believe that he was brave for her benefit.

He soon found himself strong and brave, ready to face surgery and a long recovery afterward. Each of us, too, will learn to be brave by playing with bravery. We can taste the bravery, we can feel the bravery, we can pretend the courage, and most of all we can try it out for ourselves. Having the courage to grieve leads to the courage to live, to love, to risk and to enjoy all the fruits of life without fear or inhibition. For all of us, it is our fear of loss and the sorrow of loss that keeps us from living our lives to the full.

In certain instances, our lack of awareness of grief increases our anxiety, depression, hopelessness, and helplessness when we experience a significant loss in our lives. The purpose of this book is therefore to increase our understanding and acceptance of grief as a natural, unavoidable life experience. We should all learn to trust that, while grief is painful, it is safe and surmountable, and that full grief will allow us not only to recover, but also to expand and grow. My wish is that we begin to build the courage to grieve from reading this novel.

GRIEF AND DEATH

LIVING THROUGH THE REALITY OF DEATH

Death is a natural part of life, and we behave as if death is an outrage. We see death as our enemy; we see ourselves as the future victims of death. Every body on earth is going to die. It's just a matter of time. Each one of us is like an artist working with an undefined dead-line, which is our death sentence. How do we come to embrace death as a normal thing? "If you can begin to see death as an unseen yet welcoming companion on your life's path, kindly telling you not to wait until tomorrow to do what you want to do, then you can learn to live your life instead of merely going through it."

Unfortunately, when we deny the reality of death, we find it even more terrifying and painful to face. Our own death is inconceivable. We have "a strange belief ... that we are invincible. We just can't picture ourselves dead. When you dream of death, you dream that you are a dead person and not a person who doesn't exist. "Our denial is supported by our seldom seen natural human deaths. From our point of view, several deaths take place in hospitals and nursing homes. What we see every day is violent death on television, the product of murder, fighting, and injuries. Death is dramatized as unnatural, unforeseen, and terrible.

Elisabeth Kübler-Ross writes, "In our unconscious mind we can only be killed; it is inconceivable to die of a natural cause or of old age." We also deny death by not worrying about it. We continue to share the most intertwined and evasive behaviors towards death with our most distant ancestors .... We are as displeased to learn about personal death as we are to think about it. It's an indelicacy, like talking in a mixed company about venereal disease or abortion in the old days.

Denial of death creates a lot of issues for us. It is the denial of death that is partly responsible for people living hollow, purposeless lives; for when you live as though you live forever, it is too easy to postpone things you know you have to do. You live your life in preparation for tomorrow or in memory of yesterday, and in the meantime, every one of you is lost today. If we do not reject death, we fear it. We may have a healthy regard for death or time running out of us, or we may worry too much about risk, sickness, or aging.

Some of us spend a large amount of time considering death, even terrorizing ourselves, in order to gain the upper hand over this terrifying phenomenon. Invariably, rather than becoming more strong, we make ourselves miserable. Like denial, fear of death not only makes it impossible for us to face tragedy and death in our lives, but it can keep us from living entirely, from loving, and from risking. Somewhere between the denial of death, obsessive fear of death, and thinking of suicide, there is a healthy understanding and acceptance of death as a natural phenomenon that brings context and meaning to our lives. Viktor Frankl says, "The meaning of human existence is based on its irreversible quality."

Mastery of our fear of death allows us to accept that we will die, which gives us an opportunity to make our lives more meaningful now. Expecting that we will die, we can not as easily take life for granted or push off until some unknown future. We are more capable of taking action and living our lives to the full.

Here are some truths about the phenomenon of death we need to intimate ourselves with:

1. To savor life, we need death.

2. Death is an "invention" that is required and therefore made for the sake of feeling alive.

3. Death puts us in contact with the meaning of an individual, true life.

4. Death makes possible choices about authenticity — that is, bravery and honesty.

5. Death gives us the power to make the most important choices.

6. Death exposes the importance of intimacy in life.

7. Death allows us to attribute value to our lives retroactively, a valuable idea for older people.

8. Death teaches us the value of ego-transcendent achievement.

9. Death shows us the way to self-esteem. It gives us the opportunity to do something important.

Dealing with The Death Of The Love One

No matter how it happens, the death of a loved one is devastating, traumatic, and seemingly difficult to acknowledge. Often we feel unprepared and thus saddened by death. Our loss is exacerbated by our characteristic human difficulty in separating one another; death is the supreme separation. It's not easy to face death, whatever the circumstances. Our grief may be influenced by the age and stage of our loved one's life.

We prefer to bear our suffering better when we believe that the deceased has a chance of some significant fulfillment of his or her life. The death of an infant, which seems to be the most unnatural death, is also the most anguish to face. Speaking of the death of a young person, Viktor Frankl writes, "We cannot, after all, judge a biography by its length, by the number of pages in it; we must judge by the richness of the contents…

Sometimes the 'unfinisheds' are among the most beautiful symphonies." How our loved one dies will have a profound influence on how we grieve. Sudden deaths, particularly violent or accidental deaths, are the cause of our greatest shock, anxiety and distress. Violent deaths make us feel helpless and scared. Such deaths will cause our outrage or indignation at the injustice of death. Suicide, too, has a tragic and shocking quality. Suicide can give rise to unfounded guilt or a sense of failure among the survivors. Peaceful, abrupt deaths, such as dying in one's sleep, seem more like a gift, for we think of this as an easy passage for the dead.

However, there are also questions, suspicions and worries regarding any sudden death. We're curious why the death has happened. Who is to blame for that? Would this have been prevented? Sudden deaths make you feel abnormal. We are worried about "if only," the rumors in which we attempt to rewrite history to erase this tragedy. Since we're so unprepared for loss in a sudden death, and since we usually have too much unfinished business with the dead, sudden deaths tend to be the hardest to deal with. Watching a perpetual death can also be agonizing.

Having a loved one in agony and being powerless in alleviating distress is an anguishing experience. It's also hard to live with what feels like a death sentence and then a regret, repeated over and over again, in certain long illnesses. Day-in-and-day treatment of a dying loved one can be very exhausting and stressful. Death, then, could come as a relief. Lingering deaths can be easier to cope with, though, because we have the chance to confront death and death directly. In a perpetual death, loved ones can provide warmth, support, and companionship that can relieve the pain of the dying person.

It is a profound experience for the survivor to be able to provide in this way, just as it is a great comfort for the one who is dying. To share the dying process with a loved one is to spare him or her the solitude and loneliness that are so typical of the dying process in our society. All concerned have the opportunity to be together, to deepen their affection, to express their thoughts, and to come to some kind of agreement with each other before death occurs. Any of the grievances of the survivors can be accomplished in advance of death if they are transparent and honest during this period. And the predicted death allows the dying patient a chance to complete his sorrow for his own death.

Dying is a time that calls for your active engagement in the process. Prepare yourself for a change in consciousness that is going to happen; realize what's going on in you when it happens. Read other people's experiences. Look for someone who can be with you as you make the transition represented by death, who can speak to you when you move over, who can ride most of the way with you. Share the ecstasy and enlightenment of your death with a loved one, just as you shared the exquisite joy of your birth with one or both of your parents. At least be comforted that there are people in the world who know that death is ecstasy. Why be afraid in advance of the unknown? When it becomes understood, it might not be scary at all.

It is unfortunate that so many of those dying in our country have been isolated in hospitals and nursing homes, kept away from sight, so that medical workers and families alike can escape the process of dying.

Elisabeth Kübler-Ross has been instrumental in helping to break through the denial of death in hospitals through her extensive work with the dying.

Unique Strengths Help Us Face Death

Awareness, emotional intelligence, our support system, our intent in life, and our bravery are all the qualities that allow us to cope with life and death. In certain situations, denial is just naivety, a shield against terror, but information may be the antidote to them. Information-seeking is an important part of a psychologically stable attempt to respond to a crisis situation. Educating ourselves about death will keep us from feeling depressed or devastated when we have to face the death of a loved one.

Emotional maturity is another attribute that we can use in preparing to face death. Emotional maturity is a willingness to understand and cope with reality, to experience and convey our feelings; it is also a kind of resilience, a capacity to rebound back to "natural" when faced with stress. Life constantly makes new and different demands on us, and all these demands are real opportunities for us to grow emotional maturity. Unfortunately, since we always want to escape unfamiliar or complicated or demanding circumstances, we do not often take advantage of the opportunities to improve our capacity to cope. However, at every point of our lives, the ability to mature is available to us.

Even children can cope with death with maturity if they are treated sincerely and helped in their grief. Having a life goal, giving meaning to our lives is a way to improve our daily lives and give us comfort in times of crisis. This was demonstrated dramatically by Viktor Frankl, an eminent psychiatrist who had endured the horrors of years in a Nazi concentration camp by reflecting on his life as purposeful, on his dignity as a human being, on his affection, and on what he wanted to do in the future.

Our support system is another asset that makes it easier for us to face tragedy and death. This involves the network of people and events that fill our lives, as well as the understanding and encouragement that we offer ourselves.

Finally, bravery is one of the biggest qualities we can have to face life and death. And the most defeated of us can gain bravery. Any time we're willing to take a chance, it's a step towards bravery. Whenever we have something hard to face without running away, we are brave. Having the courage to face sadness, disappointment, and suffering will always lead to a far more rewarding life. Having the courage to face death with honesty would ultimately mean that we question our lives, our beliefs, our ideas and our sense of meaning so that finally we can construct a life that has both fulfillment and intent. By acknowledging death as a normal progression of life, we can live our lives with more passion and depth, and we can reach the greatest possible richness. In other words, the willingness to embrace death would make our lives easier.

In order to build the courage to face death, most of us will need counseling to break through our own denial of death.

THE PERIOD OF MOURNING

Whenever we lose a loved one, we grieve: for weeks, for months, or even for years. This time of mourning is called the *mourning period*, first defined by Sigmund Freud in his 1917 paper "Mourning and Melancholia." While there is no fixed time, many cultures and religions signify one year of mourning. There is wisdom in the conventional one year of mourning, which allows the bereaved to take at least some of the time required to observe and complete the grieving process. In one year, we will begin to learn to cope with the absence of our loved one on any painful special occasion, such as birthdays, birthdays, and Christmas. Since grief is so painful and hard to sustain, we tend to drive ourselves to the end of mourning long before we are ready. A full year helps us to switch back and forth from our sorrow over and over again, as we aim for completion. However, a year may not be nearly enough time, and we will all recover within our own particular timeframe.

The time of mourning is just a time of convalescence. It is time to face the loss and all the emotions that the loss evokes, in order at least to begin to heal the great wound caused by the death of a loved one. This is a time when every part of our relationship with the dead — our attachment, emotions, thoughts, and memories, as well as our history, present, and future — is explored and re-examined over and over again.

The purpose of this mourning period is for us to heal, to recover, and to restore our balance and our ability to live to the full again. Even in the occasional cases where we feel prepared in preparation for the death of a loved one, we are rarely prepared for the changes that loss causes in our daily lives.

Coping with these changes is another significant task of the mourning period. Where one's life was linked to another's, there's a big difference when the other is gone. This huge loss results in less painful daily losses. One of the widows told me, "Before my husband died, everything was clearly laid out for me. Suddenly, at ninety-nine, I have nothing to do, no sense of mission.

Suddenly having to start redefining our lives and creating new meaning and intent can seem like an enormous challenge. Wounds don't recover without time and care. Yet so many of us believe like we have no right to take time to recover from emotional or psychological wounds. Ideally, we should not drive ourselves back too easily to our daily routine, lest we accentuate our pain.

However, most of us do not have the luxury of withdrawing from our obligations, so it is important that we do not expect too much of ourselves. Since loss makes life feel very abnormal, attempting to regain "natural" routine too quickly after death can be a very difficult task. There are two major psychological activities to be undertaken during the mourning period. The first is to understand and recognize the truth: that death has occurred and that the relationship is over.

The second task is to experience and cope with all the feelings and difficulties that the loss produces for the bereaved. These activities are interconnected. Each of them takes time. Each of them is important for the eventual recovery from grief. When we mourn, our sorrow is in the forefront, and most of the other facets of life pass into the background. One woman explained her experience of mourning this way: "At first, I felt like my loss was like a spotlight in front of my eyes all the time. I could see nothing but the spotlight. I've been blinded by that. As time passed, the light shifted away from my eyes, and I could see what was around and behind it. Now, months later, much of the time, the spotlight is out of reach. I know it still exists, but I'm not aware of it all the time."

Morning is a moment in life when we are able to feel like we have the freedom to set everything else aside. For many of us, the cessation of operations and the freedom to work are important and a source of great relief. We may need to do nothing for weeks, maybe for the first time in our lives. For others of us, time and activity gaps can accentuate our loss too painfully. Then we can not bear nothingness and need to continue to work in our sorrow. It's important to remember that we're not all the same about how we grieve. Just like each of us has to grieve in our own way, so our needs and responses may not be the same every time we face a loss.

Feelings of grief are very strong and sometimes mixed. We can experience emotions in a completely new or different way. Among the many emotions aroused by death are grief, sorrow, disbelief, despair, anxiety, isolation, remorse, regret, bitterness, emptiness, and numbness, as well as longing, affection, and admiration for the dead. These are all normal feelings of sadness that can occur together or at different times. It is necessary for us to understand our emotions, not to deny them, for the sake of preserving our emotional wellbeing. We must learn to tolerate and embrace our feelings as well as our own loss.

Emotional pain is not permanent, even though sometimes we believe it is. Emotional pain is persistent only when all our attention is in the process of suppressing certain emotions that are so hard to suppress. We can not withstand the relentless bombardment of emotional pain. The normal process of mourning involves enduring moments of intense emotion, accompanied by periods of silence. Allowing ourselves to move naturally in and out of pain, instead of placing rigid restraints on our emotions, helps us to go through and complete the process of grief more easily.

In other words, coping with sorrow rather than preventing it shortens the length of the trauma. Some of us have let our feelings out completely and freely, because we instinctively know that this is right for us. But without knowing why we are doing this, the majority of us feel compelled to express ourselves in this way. For others, this degree of transparency would be a new experience, maybe a challenging one, and even an incredibly difficult undertaking.

We have to understand our needs in order to mourn fully. First of all, we need to take the time to grieve. We need to talk and sob as much as we can. We need an atmosphere, or people around us, that supports our grief rather than prevents us. We need to be free from big decisions if we feel unsafe or unprepared for them. What is most difficult for all of us to mourn is that this is a moment when we instinctively need so much. It is important that we respect our needs and realize that we are not self-indulgent, but self-sustaining instead.

THE FIRST STAGE OF GRIEF: SHOCK

Until we heal from grief, we go through several different moods and emotions to cope with death and loss. There are several stages of grief between the initial disbelief and the actual recognition of death. Memories, thoughts, and emotions are gathered and relinquished again and again before mourning is over.

There are three big steps in the grieving process for most of us. The first phase is one of shock or numbness that can last for hours, days, or even weeks. The second and longest phase, which can last for months, is the period of suffering and disorganization. The last stage is the reorganization period.

"I can't believe that!" It is also our first reaction to our acknowledgement of death. The loss of a loved one is always amazing. We don't want to make death real. It's much the same as living a nightmare, because the fact of death feels unreal and impossible.

We go numb to some point when we're surprised. Then we're stuck in a state of unreality, just slightly conscious of what's going on around us. Some of our suffering is shut down, as if we were partly anesthetized.

Experience is blurred or hazy. We seem to be existing in a dream. Our whole body provides this inherent defense against the full impact of our failure at once. Just like the body goes into shock after an accident or injury, so the mind goes into shock when confronted with major emotional crises. The numbness or anesthesia is temporary.

The duration of time is uncertain, but shocks can last for days or weeks. The numbness momentarily isolates us from the strength of our emotions, but it can also prevent us from immediately understanding the full meaning of the loss. Panic often alternates with numbness. We can suddenly feel scared that we can't remember what our dead loved one looked like, or fear that we can't go on alone now. It's necessary to temper these sudden jolts, to ease us slowly to face the reality of our loss.

Thus, numbness is a requisite feature of the early days of mourning. Our numbness also helps us to cope with a multitude of information that need to be dealt with shortly after the death of a loved one. These events and the people who share our lives also keep us alive during the first days of mourning. Although the bereaved sometimes remember little of the time of shock after death, many remember their rage, which is often unreasonable and uncontrolled. While sorrow and pain are veiled in shock for us, rage can lash out openly, unexpectedly, at almost any target. Rage is one of the few outlets we have for disbelief, frustration, and helplessness that we experience when faced with death. Rage often provokes moments of life in what is normally a time of numbness.

Given the fact that indignation can feel awkward and surprising under these circumstances, we need to embrace it as normal. People in shock often appear stoic, as if they're dealing without a lot of emotion. The reality is that we do not experience the full impact of the loss in shock, and so we do not suffer like we do when the numbness is gone. Observing someone who is in great pain behaving in a stoic, seemingly emotional way can be a bewildering experience.

But this apparent stoicism is simply a robotic way of operating. Being able to work at all will reassure us that we are coping and not falling apart because of the effects of our loss. For e.g., a friend's mother chatted incessantly about inconsequential issues for days after her husband died. Finally, in complete anger, my friend begged his mother to spend some peaceful time alone with him. His mother said indignantly, "I can't be silent or I will cry."

For Diane Kennedy Pike, the wife of Bishop James Pike, it was during the moment of shock that she documented all the events that followed her husband's death in the Israeli wilderness. In reality, during the first weeks of her grief, she produced her book Quest before she fully realized her pain. And after we recover from the initial shock of loss, there will be moments in the coming days and months when we feel "I can't believe it!" again. Our psyches scrutinize the truth of death over and over, seeking to embrace and incorporate the loss into our lives.

Since death is typically a possibility that we do not want to believe, it is a long, slow process to resolve our reluctance and embrace truth. The reality is, we're all hoping we're going to wake up from this nightmare.

THE MIDDLE STAGE OF GRIEF: SUFFERING AND DISORGANIZATION

When the shock wears off, as if coming out of a trance, we begin to feel the full impact and pain of facing the finality of our loss. This is a time of immense pain. Diane Kennedy Pike characterized the loss of a loved one as having a tree growing in one's heart, unexpectedly yanked by its roots, leaving a gaping hole or a wound. The pain is severe, but it is not constant. Both the feelings that follow loss — unbalancing, daunting, and as fresh and as distinct as they may be — and the real changes in life triggered by death are disorganizing for us.

It's normal for us to weep a lot now. Tears are nature's way of helping us to communicate and relieve our pain. We could ruminate and be deeply concerned about the specifics of the lost loved one's life or death, about our relationship with each other, about our memories, about our last meeting, about our unfinished business together, or even about our more abstract ideas about death. So bewildered are we by the reality of death that many of us have been concerned for a time with profound concerns as to why the loved one died. And because grief exaggerates the positive and negative aspects of our relationship, we are able to go over and over these aspects in our minds.

Our minds can seem to work intensely quickly, covering all the specifics of the dead. One man told me after his son died that he seemed to think about his son "eight hundred times a day" at first, no matter what he was doing to keep himself occupied. Ruminating is a part of the healing process. Yet as busy as our minds may be in one way, in another way, we may feel hollow, out of space, unable to focus or concentrate. We'll hear and respond to other people often. At other times, we may feel powerless to respond to something that accentuates our sense of alienation from those around us. Emotionally, we experience acute pain, or even hysteria.

This strength of feeling could be new to us. We can find it particularly difficult to identify such emotions as resentment, rage, self-pity, and guilt. Although we may be perplexed or confused by our feelings, we need to remember that this is the way most people are affected by grief. We may feel unprepared to cope with too much emotion, or we may feel inadequate for the task. Our questions about our ability to cope can cause a temporary decrease in self-esteem, just as such uncomfortable emotions, such as remorse or anger, can cause us to feel bad about ourselves temporarily during the mourning process.

Likewise, a sense of poverty is characteristic of mourning. Therefore, our greatest need is at this difficult period of companionship. We may need others to listen to us, to speak to us, to keep us, to take over for us. This new onslaught of needs can be very uncomfortable, even terrifying, but it confirms how distinctive the grievances of normal times are.

Death is such an emotional crisis that it is normal for us to feel needy, tired, and depressed as well as unable to cope with or work for a while. If this time of need arises while we are alone and without help, our needs may seem much more acute. Depression and sorrow are inextricably related. When we grieve, we are naturally sad. Depressed, we feel irritable, dejected in spirits, withdrawn, unresponsive, apathetic, unconcentrated, powerless, and unreliable. Appetite loss and severe fatigue are also symptomatic of depression and grief. So much of our energy is tied up within that little energy is available for action or activity. We may be moody. At times we may feel pain and cry, and at other times we may feel detached and emotionless. During this time, we can be withdrawn and unable to relate to others. Negativity, pessimism, emptiness, and a fleeting feeling of life's worthlessness are all signs of depression. "What is the use of it? "Or" Why bother about it? "These are common emotions. We can be acutely restless and become immobile. Feelings differ, of course, and not everyone can feel all the emotions that have been described. The important thing to remember is that the agony of grief is never constant and never continues forever.

Throughout this middle period of grieving, a multitude of feelings of sadness come and go in waves, with less severity as time goes by. Thoughts of suicide are not uncommon when a person grieves. However, it is important to note that these are just feelings, that we are not going to act on them. The wish to die is, in part, a wish to reunite with the deceased loved one. Thoughts of death are also an imaginary way to get relief from the agony of grief. Suicide thoughts can be the product of unexpressed remorse or rage, and they act as self-punishing ideas.

Since existence does not seem to be very important at the time of mourning, it is common to see death as an alternative. Considering suicide is also one way to deal with the facts of loss and death. Thinking is something like this: if I can accept and embrace the possibility of my own death, then death itself would not seem so terrifying or so difficult for me to bear. Maybe then I'm going to embrace this defeat. When we come to recognize the loss of the loved one, the thoughts of suicide vanish.

Typically, our sleep is disturbed if we experience significant emotional crises of some sort. Almost every person who is in the midst of extreme grief has trouble sleeping. Sleep disorders are the product of the great burden of therapeutic work involved in grief. We iron out many of our psychic issues during sleep in normal periods. Grief causes an overload, more work than the mind can do comfortably, either in sleep or in waking time. Insomnia becomes very common. There are a variety of forms of insomnia. The difficulty of falling asleep is one type. Frequently, obsessive thought will hold us up. Since we always associate falling asleep with death, as we grieve, we can be afraid of falling asleep. Another form of insomnia is always staying awake, or completely awake after just a few hours of sleep, unable to sleep more. It is also normal to lament long hours of sleep and never feel completely rested.

Dreaming can also be affected during the period of mourning. Dreams are a significant way of re-experiencing and functioning through emotionally charged encounters and problem-solving. A lot of pain work is going to be done in our sleep. Unpleasant dreams or nightmares can occur at any period in our lives, but they may be more memorable or more troubling while we are grieving and vulnerable. On the other hand, not recalling dreams, not even feeling anesthetized at night, is not uncommon during mourning. After a loved one dies, it is very natural to dream of that person, sometimes as if they never died at all. Dreams often reflect our own desires. Dreaming of the loved one is another way to begin to embrace death, distressing as it is to reawaken to the fact of death. One of my clients said, "As hard as it is to dream of my dead boy, it is wonderful to be able to be with him again, at least in my sleep." It was definitely comforting to me to have some kind of interaction with my brother through dreams, long after his death.

During the time of mourning, it is necessary to rest in order to regenerate our energies, to maintain our strength and to maintain our health even if we are unable to sleep a lot. We are much more vulnerable to sickness and infection when our vitality is drained, as it is during the mourning period. Often, when we grieve, we falsely assume that we should let ourselves go physically, when in fact, the opposite is true.

We may lose interest in food. The most severe type of this is called anorexia, which is the refusal to eat. Weight loss is normal in bereavement. But we can eat more under the stress of grief, and sometimes chronic hunger continues even after feeding. We need to make sure that we have a balanced diet that contains a lot of protein. While we are in pain, we often eat badly, turning to carbohydrates and sugars, which, while immediately satisfying food, are not as nutritious as proteins. Vitamin C and the stress vitamin regimen can also help. We should consult someone who is knowledgeable about nutrition and health for further assistance in this regard.

When we are upset or nervous, we often experience physical symptoms such as dizziness, shaking, shortness of breath, headaches, heartburn, and new aches and pains, as well as exhaustion that is characteristic of grief. Some of the mourners appear to have a constant cold. These are stress reactions related to sleep problems that are typical of the time of mourning.

We can also become obsessively worried with our health and body functions after a loved one dies, which is also a natural outgrowth of grief. Facing death will raise the consciousness of all our fears of death. Some of us may experience symptoms that resemble the illness of the deceased on a temporary basis.

Sexuality is also greatly influenced by grief. After the death of a partner, sexual frustration can be an intense cause of anguish. But there is also a natural emotional detachment during mourning, which can lead to a decrease or complete loss of interest in sex. Often the enjoyment of intimacy may give rise to guilt or anxiety in the early weeks of mourning, or we may find that our sexual needs are heightened together with our other needs.

Confusion reigns when we are torn between need and desire for closeness on the one hand, and isolation and lack of sexual responsiveness on the other. Masturbation can help to alleviate sexual stress and dissatisfaction. Sexual dysfunctions of various kinds, such as impotence and premature ejaculation in men, and inability to respond or achieve orgasm in women, occur during the early months of bereavement. Symptoms in the sensitive field of sexuality generally go hand in hand with awareness, tolerance, and composure. Anyone who grieves gradually recovers sexuality, but the recovery time is variable.

Loneliness and longing are typical to bereavement. Death leaves a void in life that we feel very strongly about. At first, it's natural to think that no one — nothing — can ever fill that gap. Every person we love is special to us. The absence is felt all the more deeply because of the specialness of the loved one and our connection with each other. Death may also have left us with new obligations that were already dealt with by the deceased.

Each of these new jobs can increase our loneliness and sense of loss. We also wish that death was a lie, a mistake. We may yearn for the dead to return to us and for life to return to "normal." Isolation, as painful as it is, suggests that we are enabling ourselves to accept the reality. In coping with death, we periodically suffer from isolation, yearning, and experiencing the painful void in our lives. As we recover, these feelings decrease and gradually vanish.

The feeling of abandonment is one of the most agonizing feelings we have to experience and overcome in grief. Whatever the circumstances, we prefer to experience the death of a loved one as abandonment. Our imaginations are playing with the notion that "if he loved me, he wouldn't have died." Temporarily, we feel deserted, rejected, and unloved. Often we feel overwhelmed by feelings of worthlessness that seem to justify our loved ones leaving us.

Guilt and the accompanying self-reproach are invariably emotions that we have to face. After a loss, we are so vulnerable to guilt that we can turn every thought, emotion, experience, or recollection into guilt. Some of us are obsessed with remorse, and others feel a faint sense of guilt. Guilt will help to deny the fact of death. Being a "survivor" induces shame. We think in our minds, "Why am I here in this world, and not him?" Then we all feel blessed, afraid, relieved, and sorry at once. These mixed emotions in the depths of sorrow confuse us and trigger self-reproach.

If we've really survived a situation where others have died, such as in an accident or a battle, we're capable of experiencing a deep trauma. Besides the extreme remorse of the survivor, we may have been consumed with anger, depression , and anxiety for several months. Psychotherapy may be required to help the survivor recover. Another painful form of guilt may come after death has given us some sort of relief.

This can happen particularly when the relationship with the loved one was somehow complicated, or when the deceased was sick for a long time before he died. We may have wished for a respite from the dying process, and when death comes, we are naturally relieved. Often, too, we feel bad about the last hours, days, or weeks of the relationship. We may instantly regret a word spoken or something unsaid or undone.

We may recall the minute specifics of the last encounter, and we may be tormenting ourselves with concern for them. Or maybe we'll regret something we've done or something we've neglected to do. For example, a few people shared with me their shame of not being able to be frank with the dying person and tell him that this was really the end. Any weakness in the relationship can cause us to bet on ourselves.

Later, several kinds of unfinished business with the deceased emerge in the form of remorse. During grief, "should" and "if only" rise to the surface. Some of us are endlessly tormenting ourselves with these problems. Yet every thinking we have can be converted into a "if only" argument. Here are some sorts of "if only" that may accompany the death of a loved one, depending on the relationship and circumstances of death:

- ➢ If only I knew that she was dying ...
- ➢ If I had just made him stop smoking ...
- ➢ If only I forbade her to drive ...
- ➢ If only he hadn't made that trip ...
- ➢ If I had just gone with her ...

Then there's the "if only" to alter reality:

- ➢ If only I hadn't fought so hard with him about the money ...
- ➢ If only I would have been more caring ...
- ➢ If we didn't just pass ...

- ➢ If only he hadn't already retired ...

- ➢ If only we had more kids ...

- ➢ If I had just been stricter ...

- ➢ If only I hadn't been nagging him ...

Everything can become an "if only." Our unfulfilled desires, as well as our failures, can cause us much pain. But when we imagine that if we had behaved differently, we would have avoided death, we figuratively endowed ourselves with superhuman abilities to alter our fate. How unrealistic we are to be burdened with an inhuman liability for death. Yet, to some degree, we all do this. For a while, each of us is persuaded that changing our actions might have changed the truth. All facing a loss has some "if only." But, our shame is an exercise in futility. We can't go backward. Instead, we have to let go and forgive ourselves.

If the "if only" becomes obsessive and persists for years, the survivor suffers from a pathological problem. Some survivors are so haunted by death that they keep imagining and rearranging the entire past of the deceased, as though the survivor could stack cards in a direction other than death. Obsessively recreating the life and death of the dead is a way to ignore reality.

Guilt feelings also occur because we were not present at the time of death. We may feel robbed with the loved one of our last moments. It is a deep sorrow to think that we have let the loved one down in some big way, that our presence may have eased their death.

There may be an omnipotence fantasy implicit in this guilt: "If I had been there, he/she would not have died." This assumption counteracts the overwhelming sense of impotence that we experience when a loved one dies. Unsolved remorse is common in grief. Dealing with guilt is important, since guilt can weaken self-confidence and hinder recovery. Guilt could also be paralyzing. We must encourage ourselves to convey loudly the variations of guilt and also the stories that underpin our guilt in order to let it go.

We ought to strive for a more rational understanding of both the relationship with the deceased and death. Guilt is the emotional area in which we are most often stuck during the mourning process. It can continue because of our lack of willingness to discuss the issue with someone else. It is legitimate and always necessary for us to seek professional assistance with these sentiments.

The worst thing we can do is avoid addressing feelings of remorse, as many physical and emotional issues can result from stifling these emotions. Rage, and the resulting desire to blame others, is also a common emotion during the mourning process. We may be angry with the universe because we have had to endure this loss. "Why me, huh? "We're asking. We may envy someone who seems to be content or anyone who has never had to face such a serious loss. This new rage can be scary, and we may feel bad about being angry.

Anger can recur again and again throughout the time we grieve. Rage is the inevitable outgrowth of our sense of impotence and helplessness, our sense of disappointment and loss, and our sense of alienation of the loved one. Granger E. Westburg, in his book *Good Grief*, explains the problems that occur in anger.

When we've had something precious stripped from us, we're naturally going through a stage where we're very critical of everything, and of all those who were connected to the loss. In our systematic analysis of the case, we spare no one trying to understand why this thing happened, and who is to blame. The human is still looking for someone to blame ... we're hostile to the doctor because he worked; or we're hostile to him because he didn't function. It was wrong, no matter what he did. When we're in this mood, we're looking at all of them with ember eyes.

Often we are unable to feel anger clearly and openly. Psychologists agree that, in many instances, depression is rage that has been turned inward to oneself instead of turning outward to the true source of the universe. All of us are more comfortable getting upset than being mad. Often we have frozen frustration or indignation. Unable to face or express rage, we control it and keep it to such a degree that we feel blocked and frozen. Indications of frozen anger or rage may be behaving in word and emotion, and feeling tight, immobile, and unmoved, in a state of detachment.

The best way to deal with emotions is to express them loudly rather than hide them. Expressing feelings aloud would make them open so they can be dealt with and resolved rather than allowed to smolder inside of us and poison us. Some of us are restraining all our sadness as well as our rage and looking frozen or wooden, causing psychological paralysis for ourselves. Mourners who limit their emotions too tightly can appear paralyzed.

We may not be able to weep because we fear self-pity or "break-down" and are unable to function. Generalized fearfulness is also a normal feeling after the death of someone close to you. We might be afraid to be alone. Many newly bereaved find that home alone is at first unbearable. Fear of loss is common to you. Suddenly, the world around us is becoming fragile, and everyone we love seems to be in danger of dying at any moment. Feeling abandoned, we're afraid of desertion.

Fearing disease or injury to ourselves or to other loved ones is normal, as is fearing that we or anyone we love will unexpectedly die without warning. All these fears are the product of the shock of facing death. The world seems temporarily less secure and more threatening as we move to habituate ourselves to the loss. These worries tend to go on as we come to accept the loss more and more. Fears that continue for months after the time of loss may suggest deeper problems. Counseling or psychotherapy may be beneficial in this situation.

Ambivalence is another emotion that might occur when a loved one dies. Very seldom do we experience a kind of emotion when we're in love. Usually, in our relationships, we maintain the full expression of what we admire and what we dislike about others. When death happens, all our feelings — both positive and negative — are likely to increase and grow rapidly to the surface. This experience can be both disconcerting and overwhelming.

Positive and negative emotions are part of all of our relationships. Most of us will embrace these ambivalent feelings as very normal, even when death happens. Then we want all our negative feelings to disappear. But the only way to get feelings away is to deal with them head-on — to address them, consider them, embrace them, and then let them go.

During grief, we always strive to deny our ambivalent feelings and instead idealize the lost one. At first, we are just conscious of how great our loss is. We only remember the positive stuff and deny that we had any bad feelings about the dead. However, common idealization is a way to deny feelings such as indignation, ambivalence, and guilt. Carried for so long, this denial makes it harder to deal with the loss and recover. Instead, we must encourage ourselves to remember everything about our dead loved one, even though selective memory is very tempting.

Preoccupation with the past or the future is common in the period of mourning. The moment, fraught with agony and grief, feels like something to escape. The past is when we were all in love with our loved one, and it holds dear memories. The future, uncertain as it is, is open to our daydreams and hopes as well as our worries and doubts. We also interact with the future, falsely thinking that we can monitor it in anticipation.

Another challenging part of the grieving process is our normal conduct. We are not able to consider change easily while we grieve.

As a result, we sometimes maintain the patterns that preceded death. One of the widows told me how she kept setting the table for two, even though she was alone now. Embarrassed at first, she decided to do it deliberately for a couple of weeks before it wasn't that hard for her to eat alone. Such examples of continuing relationships include the procurement of the preferred food of the deceased, the appointment of the deceased, or the automatic participation of the deceased in any social commitment. It's as if we're momentarily forgetting about death. Several mothers described continuing to clean their dead child's room as normal, unable to dismantle or remove anything that was part of their habit of living together. Breaking the patterns that intertwined our lives with the dead, like other facets of healing from grief, is a complicated process that takes time.

It is also difficult to separate ourselves from the symbols of the loved one who is gone. Reminders seem to live everywhere and emerge when we least expect them. Symbols are difficult to deal with since they inevitably re-open the wound of loss, if only for a moment.

Frequently, during this time of mourning, we can feel unreasonable, mentally ill, or unbalanced. We say or do or imagine out-of-ordinary things and think we're going to be "crazy." It's not a mental disorder. It's a normal part of grief. In the months following the death of a loved one, we are always very out of control. Life is askew, and our feelings and actions might seem odd to us. We can experience new emotions, powerful mixtures of emotions that burst out unexpectedly. At times, even months after our loss, we can feel hysteric. Racing thoughts, frustration, inability to "think straight" or focus, anxiety, and irrational thoughts about suicide, death, or reunion with the dead all contribute to the pain and depression of mourning. Again, these are common and fleeting moments in the grievance phase.

One dramatic example of this disorganized element of grief was a woman named Margaret who got drunk some months after her husband died. Margaret phoned a close friend and expressed concern that her husband had not yet come home from work, that he was very late. Shocked that Margaret could so utterly deny her husband's death with alcohol, the friend went to Margaret and told her again that her husband was dead.

We always imagine seeing the deceased loved one on the street, and we take off chasing the stranger as if our loved one had returned. It is definitely troubling that we seem to be able to completely forget that a person is dead. This can make us feel "mad" for the moment, but what's going on is identical to what's going on in our dreams that reject death. Our minds are struggling to deal with the loss trauma. For the time being, our wish or our rejection is greater than our recognition of truth. This temporary blindness to the facts is a common part of grief.

In a similar way, during the off-balance period of mourning, we often do self-destructive acts without even being aware of what we do. Injuries and injuries, such as falls or car collisions, are characteristic of this kind of self-destructiveness during the mourning period. One woman I know broke her right hand in an accident right after her husband died.

Loss triggers enough regret without making decisions that goes beyond our control. This is especially true of big decisions, such as moving or selling major properties. The tendency under the burden of grief is to get rid of the place or stuff that reminds us of the missing loved one. Usually, we may not like our home in mourning because of the absence of a loved one. However, it might be pleasing in time to live in a place where we have memories that we treasure. Later, we might even wish to have the belongings of the loved one that were too hard to behold earlier. A lot of people come to regret that they gave up those things early in their grief. It is therefore critical that we delay decisions of this kind wherever possible. Put the things back, out of reach, to be dealt with after healing from grief.

But friends and family can be of assistance in taking decisions for the deceased in important ways: for example, by allowing the person mourning to postpone his or her return to work or school, to take the required holiday, or to put off disposing of the deceased's belongings. Often, a supportive motivation to carry on with life may be a crucial factor in the recovery from grief.

The picture we have of ourselves throughout our grief appears to slip between two extremes. We may feel like someone "extra," but it is more likely that we will respond to the wound of sorrow with the feeling that we are the victim of disaster or loss, of abandonment, or even of fate. Since we feel like a survivor, we may feel handicapped by the strength of our pain and sorrow. The universe reinforces our feeling of becoming victims in a number of ways. We're feeling sorry. People are heading towards us and away from us in new and different ways. We're being overlooked.

47

We're getting heard. We get so much attention, too many questions are asked, too frequently, too much for comfort.

Conversely, we still feel "special" when we grieve. The universe appears to be stopping for us. People are waiting for us or trying to fulfill many of our regular needs, which nobody even seemed to realize before. Demands on us to decrease or to stop. We're receiving phone calls, visits, presents, letters. New people often reach out to us. We feel very necessary and cared for. This unique care is very compassionate. It could be the only thing that can help us as we face the agony of our grief.

When the world resumes and we are no longer regarded as "special" there is almost always a major, though temporary, emotional change. People seem to be abruptly and arbitrarily withdrawing from the bereaved, as if the time for mourning was over and we were supposed to resume our regular lives. This experience was defined by a man whose wife had been dead for five months. "Just a few people are calling me now. Well, I'm really lonely. No one is worried about my meals or how I handle my time. People abruptly vanished, believing that I was completely healed from my loss. Well, I'm not recovered. My isolation seems much worse now. I 'm ashamed that I miss feeling special." So, it's important to comfort the bereaved not to pull out our support too quickly or without warning.

Occasionally, some of us become so attached to this special treatment that we hang on to our sorrow in order to keep our focus going or to delay the resumption of our lives. Unfortunately, disaster is one of the key ways to be heard and cared for in our society. It takes courage to risk seeking more constructive ways of communicating with others, just as it takes courage to restart life independently.

In this age, dying is more difficult for the bereaved, since they are more alone and there are less funeral ceremonies and practices than in earlier days. People without a sustained belief system or clear religious beliefs and relationships often feel confused and lonely.

Many of them turn to faith effectively for consolation. Death is a mystery that poses metaphysical issues. We wonder if there is a Heaven, and what's really going to happen after death. We're just asking "Why me? "Or why did he die? "The hunt for deeper answers to these unknowns is part of the quest of the most grieving people.

THE LAST STAGE OF GRIEF: AFTERSHOCKS AND REORGANIZATION

After several months, when the reality of death has deepened, our desires and the pace of our lives start to shift. We are entering a new era of grievance, the reorganization age. During this next point, we seem to respond differently. We may need more quiet and less people around, when we have not been able to be alone so far. If we have been very quiet and withdrawn, we might be able to resume a more involved social life. It could be harder to just sit around now. We may feel more urgent about filling the void the loss has created in our lives. We can need more activity, more participation in life. However, our desire to express ourselves continues in the mourning period, whether we respect the need or not.

We can see that we are getting closer to healing from grief when the deceased is no longer our primary concern. In time, this transition happens naturally, but it can be distressing rather than welcoming if we falsely assume that our love of the dead is determined by the intensity of our sorrow. It is necessary to clear ourselves of such myths so that we can fully reorganize our lives.

As our sense of loss decreases from extreme sorrow to mild sorrow, our appetite, sleep, energy, and functioning are almost returned to "normal." Likewise, we become more involved in the world and in increasing our activities. At this moment, a big shift is that we are more attracted to our own future. We're beginning to reinvest ourselves in our lives. Now we're going to have a future, and we're beginning to get involved in building our life ahead.

We know we're not going to forget the one who died, but the individual shifts from the foreground to the background. We need to talk less often about the deceased, and we are less worried about the possessions, memories, and stories of the deceased loved one. Loss is no less true, but our sense of impoverishment is diminishing. Once again, we begin to feel whole and a sense of "normality." In this reorganization process, months after our loss, we can believe that we are healing from our grief because we have more energy and feel more able to cope with it.

This may not be valid. And though we feel much better, we might still be working through our grief as deeply as before, but in more subtle, less noticeable ways. This could be a time of aftershocks in the form of unforeseen jolts of disturbed feelings or unexpected reminders of our loss and grief. For example , a young widow who was ready to enjoy herself and even to love again went out on a date several months after her husband's death.

Suddenly, after a drink, she found herself crying with the new man she wanted to impress. Lynn Caine in *Widow* spoke about moving to the suburbs, an impulsive move that turned out to be devastatingly miserable for herself and her children. And an easygoing woman named Alice suddenly found herself angry at a friend who worried about her teenage daughter, when all Alice could think about was her desolation that she had no daughter at all. Even though our re-entry and re-investment in living starts to reorganize, our continued internal grievance mechanism prevents us from feeling fully "natural" yet.

While we are now starting to completely let go of the dead, this resolution does not always happen automatically or naturally. Often we need to solidify the process of letting go of it. We will need a sense in which we let go, be it a ceremony or a set time, or a plan to say good-bye.

Our convictions are impacting our mourning. If we believe in life after death, in heaven, or in rebirth, it is always easier to think about letting the dead go. Resolution can take longer, however, if we agree that the good-bye we have to say is permanent. Whatever our values, we may try to say good-bye to the image or memory of the deceased and imagine that the loved one is floating up into the vast universe to help us give our good-bye a solid shape. This could be a serious start to let go. Acknowledging good-bye out loud could be especially helpful. Of course, even after the full thrust of mourning is complete, there can be tough days. Anniversaries or reminders can give rise to grief again for a moment. The re-emergence of grief at this time is a common part of coming to terms with the recognition of the loss of a loved one.

UNSUCCESSFUL GRIEF

Healthy grief, dramatic and even painful as it may be, is a three-stage phase. First of all, it is thoroughly feeling and voicing all the feelings and reactions to the loss. Second, it's going to complete and let go of the attachment to both the dead and the sorrow. Third, it is recovering and re-investing in one's own life. Failure to take some steps in the grieving process may result in an unhealthful or ineffective grievance. Since these stages may take several months to complete, the inadequate grief may not appear until long after the loss has occurred. However, as even failed complaints become clear, they can be explored and resolved successfully. Unsuccessful grief is normally reversible.

For us to complete every step of the mourning process involves understanding, bravery, openness, self-help and the support of others. Due to the difficulty of this process, many of us do not completely complete every required step. That's why unlucky or unhealthful sorrow is popular. Further complicating our completion of the mourning process is the fact that our reaction to loss is always automatic or unconscious, so that we may be unaware of what we are going through.

Since the mourning process is largely learned, few of us experience a healthy grievance without first using more unsuitable means to cope with our pain and sorrow. We are more likely to cope with death effectively because we have learned to deal with loss and separation earlier. Each of us will possibly find some common examples of unsuccessful grief. The goal here, however, is to provide understanding and advice for dealing with future grievances rather than chastising ourselves for earlier failures.

Of the many causes of inadequate grief, the most basic is our lack of awareness about witnessing and completing the period of mourning. Unconscious about how we can effectively grieve, we continue to deny, postpone, hinder, or displace our feelings. Indirectly conveyed or unexpressed sorrow is unhealthful. The other extreme — exaggerating or prolonging our sorrow for years after the real loss — is often unhealthful.

This happens when we over-idealize the deceased, or hold on to emotions like sadness or remorse, or refuse to completely regain our lives after the loss. Many of us falsely believe that if we really loved, we will never end up in sorrow. Long, unsolved grief is seen as a declaration of love rather than what it really is — pathological grief. The more mature our relationship with the deceased was, the greater chance we have of a healthy solution to our grief.

Unsuccessful sorrow is often the product of stereotypes of bravery throughout our culture. For example, bravery is also seen as a capacity to remain quiet while in pain, to suppress tears at all costs, to act independently of the depths of chaos inside us, and to deal with our wounds and sorrows privately and independently. None of us are superhuman.

Typically, as we want to live according to these values, we deny our suffering and never learn to cope with it. Since unexpressed pain does not vanish spontaneously, we will have serious consequences if we claim to be superhuman. A severe example of this was Rachael, whose husband died suddenly in the early sixties. From the day of her death, Rachael never mentioned her husband, never shedding a tear. She had signs of senility within a year. Another example of massive self-control was George, who appeared stoically to face the death of his son without crying. Yet, six months later, George died of a heart attack.

Both Rachael and George suffered horrific effects as a result of their enormous influence over their feelings of grief. While we can feel "crazy" or out of control while we grieve, few of us truly lose our hold on reality for any extended period of time. But if we force ourselves to contain our sorrow or deny our loss, we can lose control of our mental faculties.

This is an unhealthful condition that might require medical treatment or hospitalization to allow us the opportunity to grieve and reorganize. It takes a great deal of strength to experience pain openly and frankly, to sit in the midst of such painful thoughts and reactions until we have shared them and finished them. It takes bravery to be able to completely endure the agony and sorrow of grief and to confront emotions at the moment they arise rather than prolong the encounter.

The most serious type of unexpressed grief is absent grief. The death of a loved one is such a shock that at first, we sometimes go numb and have no reaction at all for a short time. However, having no response to the death of a loved one a few weeks or months later may be symptomatic of pathological grief. Repressing a big emotional onslaught, like grief, may have an impact on our emotional and physical wellbeing. The repression of grief can incapacitate us by causing our emotions to be deadened or distorted, our relationships to suffer, and our functioning to be impaired.

A word of advice about absent grief: sometimes we just don't have any grief. This could happen when we finally resolved the relationship with the deceased before death, or when we didn't have a major emotional interest in the person who died. Some profoundly spiritual people instinctively and positively embrace death and thus do not grieve. And older people, who have had more experience with death, may be more likely to accept loss. When a long illness followed the death of a loved one, the pain may have been dealt with in advance. And some people are grieving in secret. Such a private grievance is not to be confused with a lack of sorrow.

Denial of grief is similar to absent grief. Overwhelmed by the defeat, we are seeking to delay the reality of death. Some denial is common in the process of getting used to loss, but denial as one's only tool for coping is unhealthful. Denial of grief typically appears in the disguise of claim not to care, rather than in the absence of true emotions. For example, a child's assertion that he or she does not feel something when he or she is obviously moody, pessimistic, or withdrawn suggests a denied reaction. Adults often behave the same way, or they can become very busy covering up their sorrow. Denial can be a delicate defense that others can crack through with honesty and kindness of encouragement.

Grief is inhibited when a bereaved person, or someone close to him, cuts off the normal flow of the feelings of loss. Fear of emotions or their strength, discomfort with tears, and false confidence in silence and self-control are all factors that prevent grief. We are forced to be inhibited by our sorrow and unable to complete it if we can not express our feelings.

The feelings of grief persist and surface in some other way later. Delayed grief is the denial of emotions at the crucial early stages of grieving to be dealt with at some future time. Sometimes we lack the strength to face grievances at their strongest, and we believe that delaying grievances would make it easier later. Often, too, we pause in order to preserve our functioning or to comfort someone else who is mourning at the same time. If the desire to extend grief is intentional or unconscious, delayed grief is simply a bottled-up pain that will explode with its original intensity at some later time or in some other part of our lives.

Delaying grief always leaves us vulnerable to an unforeseen emotional outburst. There is a great deal of evidence of unsuccessful or inhibited grief. Sudden changes in personality and progressive social isolation after loss can lead to unsolved grief. The bereaved may become apathetic or unusually circumscribed and cautious. In managing their emotions, particularly unsolved animosity, the bereaved may become "wooden and formal." There may be a reluctance to speak about the deceased or even to mention his or her name. Likewise, emotionally charged conversational subjects are apt to avoid. The inhibited survivor may refuse to understand feelings or may often face sadness from an analytical rather than an emotional point of view. Death may be referred to casually or not at all. Non-verbal clues to inhibited grief include visible body stress, stiff posture, taut neck, strained or brittle smile, loss of eye contact, strained movements such as pacing or finger tapping, or withdrawal of behaviour.

Whether or not we are mindful of it, we pay an immense price for inhibiting sorrow. Often the price is a lack of our zest for life, which can persist for months or even years. After we have suffered a loss that we have not completely mourned, we may withdraw from others or decide that closeness is not worth the effort. We can simply get into a life pattern of overwork in order to prevent us from avoiding it. Others of us will need a few drinks to get through the day or dependent on drugs or drugs. Promiscuity, heavy gambling, and other compulsive habits may be subject to unsolved sorrow. Constant colds or other persistent physical symptoms may be the price that we pay for inhibiting our grief. Death or suicide is another potential symptom of unexpressed sorrow.

Many encounters can cause a grievance that was ignored earlier. This may involve a different loss, a different kind of upset in our lives, a new event like the birth of a child, the reappearance of an old friend or an old memory, a film, a book, and particularly a significant anniversary or date in our own life or that of the deceased. "Anniversary reactions"—one or even fifty years after death — are normal to most of us, whether we are completely grieved or not. Anniversaries are all the more strong because our emotions about the loss have been suppressed. We may be shocked at a time that may seem inappropriate, or when there is no help from others. There are times when most of us need some support in completing the grieving process; usually, this help will come from a specialist. In my experience, the majority of people come for psychotherapy for the first time because of earlier grief that is impacting their lives.

Typical events of life, such as graduation, marriage, or the birth of a child, frequently lead to sorrow for a deceased parent, grandparent, or sibling who had not only missed the occurrence but had perhaps never had the opportunity for the same experience. Other traumas, such as a car accident, illness or job loss, can precipitate unsolved grief.

Whenever the grievance is found to be unresolved, it is time to deal with it, and it is never too late to express the grievance and complete the grievance phase. Typically the dilemma emerges because the victim had to face the feelings of loss on his own in the first place, but obviously the bereaved now should not attempt to go on their own. A professional psychologist or therapist who can help us cope with the loss, and any emotions that have not been addressed should be found.

Exaggerated sorrow, or chronic bereavement — the opposite of unexpressed grief— is often unhealthful. This is the sadness that remains prevalent in our lives years after the loss of life. Significant here is how long the grievance has been going on. Other signs are morbid brooding and continued attempts to reunite with the deceased even after death. Similarly, becoming too worried with the deceased loved one rather than redefining priorities and reinvesting pathological actions in our lives.

Some clues to recurrent grief are the deceased in the present tense as if he or she were living, and the overvaluing of items and concepts that belonged to the deceased.

Excessive bereavement is generally accepted by the public, since ongoing grief is always so moving. Instead of seeing it as pathological, we prefer to romanticize excessive sorrow. We also accept such grief because we don't know what to do to motivate others to complete the grievance process. Something significant is lacking from the mourning process of a person who has not been able to overcome a death after several years. It's unhealthful for a survivor to cling to a loss; ultimately, he or she has to let go. Hidden emotions, too difficult to face, are always the root cause of prolonged sorrow. Any feelings could fall into this category, but most of us find it especially difficult to accept our ambivalence, anger, and remorse towards a loved one who dies. We thus continue to exist in the midst of the strength of our grief, in order to block the other unacceptable emotions. At times, we prolong our grief because of our intense reliance on the deceased, to prevent taking fresh, independent action in our lives.

Often our fears in life are more difficult to face than our sorrow, which is now well established. Fear of new relationships, sexuality, obligation, and change may prevent us from completing the grieving process. Finally, when grief has given us more support and attention from others than we have ever received before, it can be painfully difficult to let go of the special care given to us as the bereaved. Hanging on to some single memory, feeling, or idea years after a loss is often unhealthful. Since life naturally involves continuous change, our attachment to the past hinders our development. For example, Paul is a man who, twenty-five years after his son's death, still regrets not having helped him choose another college.

This method of analyzing and rewriting history years later is a way of holding on to the past and shows ineffective grievances. As all other signs of mourning, obsessive thought about the deceased is typical of the first months of mourning and is abnormal if it lasts years after the usual mourning era. Guilt is one of the most common and painful emotions that can interfere with the successful completion of grief. Too much we are unable to forgive ourselves for years after the mistake we have made, or even when we are blameless. Our lack of self-forgiveness perpetuates the mourning process. Parents, for example, appear to feel unnecessarily guilty for a child who dies, regardless of circumstances, and to blame themselves unfairly, as though they were somehow incompetent. Similarly, sticking to an unfulfilled pledge provided by the deceased suggests a lack of resolution of the grievance. For example, Esther, whose husband died leaving her with young children, had been resentful for years that he had broken his pledge to help raise their two sons.

Whenever "if only" remains years after loss, the sorrow is clearly not resolved. Professional support is definitely needed because we are likely to be unable to face the requisite grief work on our own. Overidealization of the deceased, which occurs after the first year or so of mourning, is typically symptomatic of unsuccessful grief. In certain instances, the one we loved becomes all the more wonderful when we're parted.

Without the presence of a loved one in our everyday lives, we might forget the stuff that upset or frustrated us. Focusing solely on the optimistic and idealizing of the loved one often helps us to deny uncomfortable emotions such as disappointment, ambivalence and guilt. Over-idealization can also suggest our inability to return to reality.

However, romanticizing the dead simply causes more issues for us by making fact seem all the more hollow compared to the idealized past. Elina was a woman who basically built a shrine for her deceased husband, which consisted of photos and other memorabilia. When the visitors arrived, she behaved as if she had expected them to participate in worship at the shrine. Most ironic was the fact that her deceased husband was a very shady businessman, in comparison to the god she created when he died.

In addition to exaggerated and underexpressed grief, there are symptoms that signify unsuccessful grief, the most common of which are fearfulness, anxiety, depression, and psychosomatic symptoms. Since depression and grief seem identical, it is important to be able to differentiate between the two. In both cases, one is capable of experiencing loss of appetite, weight loss, insomnia, lack of sexual desire, and self-denial. However, if these symptoms continue after a year of mourning, the chances are that the person is depressed.

Instead of being preoccupied with the deceased, the depressed person appears to be more preoccupied with self, to blame self, and to refer to themselves as "evil" rather than bereaved. Freud delineated depression or melancholy by the extreme decline in self-esteem. We appear to be compassionate to someone who is grieving, and more annoyed to someone who is unhappy. The grieving person always reacts, relates, and even laughs at times, while the depressed person is generally humorless and dissatisfied.

Psychological and often antidepressant treatment are ways to help resolve depression. Anxiety or fearfulness that continues well past the experience of loss is another indication of unsuccessful grief. General tenseness, trouble focusing, stage fright, unorganic sweatiness, facial flushing, and heart palpitations are indicators of anxiety. Death and loss will shake us to the very core. If we do not allow deep feelings to emerge as we grieve, our bottled-up feelings can make us tense or nervous. Often our fear is a way of expecting a loss of life. Unexpected deaths, in particular, take us off balance, leaving us vulnerable and powerless. We often put ourselves on guard after such a loss, knowingly or not, as if we might avoid further attacks on our emotions.

Fearfulness is an exaggerated form of fear. Fear of the loss of other loved ones is normal after we have suffered one loss. We can find ourselves obsessively watching every step that a surviving child or a spouse makes. We're afraid that the trauma is going to be replicated. Trying to suppress our worries also makes them worse, producing a vicious cycle. Again, a competent psychologist will help us conquer our doubts and resolve the constant sadness that lies behind them. Often we are unaware of the link between our fears and our unsolved grief. This was the case with Helen, a former client of mine.

Hilda was chronically reluctant to fly. She was reluctant to leave her house and did so just to attend her twice-weekly care appointments. She declined to ride by car, so she would walk a number of blocks to the clinic. When we started out together, she had had a few years of failed counseling with a long line of therapists. As far as I am concerned, the most important thing about Hilda's history was that she had been on an exciting car ride across the United States when her mother suddenly died. Since Hilda was out of control, traveling without a scheduled itinerary, she didn't hear the news until after the funeral. Not only was Hilda unable to be with her mother when she died, she also missed the funeral and shared the grief with the rest of her family. Hilda was overcome with remorse and sorrow that she had traveled and had fun when her mother would have needed her. She agreed unintentionally that she would never fly again as a defense against future tragedies in her life and as a punishment for herself. Hilda's remorse was intensified by ambivalent feelings about her mother, feelings that are common for most of us. It was also difficult for her to give up her guilt. But once she had completely acknowledged her feelings and learned to forgive herself, her travel phobia had vanished. Hilda's reaction may seem childish to some of us, but it demonstrates that a tragic loss of life may cause our most primal reactions. Suppressing these can lead to a neurotic symptom, such as Hilda's, or anxiety, or depression, or a physical symptom. In order to prevent such reactions, we need to express our feelings freely rather than hide them. Fear of death is a simple and typical symptom of unsolved grief.

Mabel was thirteen when her mother died from cancer. Since Mabel had not been told of her mother's imminent death, she developed the fear of facing an unexpected death that had lasted for years. Mabel was afraid to close her eyes at night, lest she should wake up. She was scared that she would be hurt or killed if she wanted to take part in sports or other physical activities. She was afraid to ride a car, and she never ventured into a plane. She watched her body attentively for some indication of life-threatening disease, like that of her mother. Mabel was so consumed with thoughts of her own death that she was less and less able to work or even venture out of her home. Luckily, the school counselor sensed Mabel's need for support. As Mabel eventually resolved her shock and grief, her symptoms and fears vanished.

Hypochondria, like fears of death, is common during mourning and is pathological when carried outside the confines of the initial period of mourning. Anxiety regarding one 's wellbeing without a real basis, or the development of fictional disorders, is characteristic of the hypochondriac. For example, in someone who is concerned with illness and death, a headache may signify a brain tumor…It is normal to mimic the illness suffered by the deceased. For example, if a loved one died of cancer, the survivor might imagine or be worried about symptoms that could suggest cancer. It is easier for all of us to pay attention to physical rather than emotional pain.

We may also be more at ease in enlisting support from others for physical rather than emotional issues. Often the stress of grief causes serious physical issues in the bereaved person, or it can worsen a pre-existing physical or emotional issue. In an important psychological study, Erich Lindemann was concerned that illnesses such as asthma, migraines, colitis, and arthritis, as well as emotional disorders, could evolve in order to prevent pain. So, if the symptoms seem true or imaginary, it's a good idea to consult a physician to be sure of that.

Grief may become somatic and transform into a real physical illness. Disease then serves as a replacement for unsolved grief. The loss of a loved one, if not successfully mourned and resolved, can precipitate a serious, perhaps life-threatening, illness. A psychiatrist David Peretz suggests that , "It has been postulated that depression and/ or marked feelings of helplessness lower resistance to infection and perhaps even reduce the body's immune defense." Carl and Stephanie Simonton, pioneering researchers on the topic of psychological factors in cancer, concur, noting that high levels of stress and chronic stress — which is what unsolved grief becomes.

Loss can lead to a wide variety of psychological and physical problems. Because grief and unanswered grief are such prevalent human issues, we need to be understanding, accommodating, and conscious of the difficulties each of us has in completing the grievance phase. We must also note that any time the grief is uncovered, it can be overcome successfully.

IS IT POSSIBLE TO DIE OF A BROKEN HEART?

Researchers who study how our behavior, emotions, and social environments affect our immune system are referred to as psychoneuroimmunology (pronounced sigh ko noo row imm you no low gee) researchers. These scientists help us realize that it is not being bereaved on its own that causes medical problems. Rather, it is the change in your conditions and actions that may cause you medical issues. For example, if you lose your partner and now have to live on your own, social isolation can be detrimental to your health. Or, you could not eat enough, and that might exacerbate diabetes or a heart disease. Or, you might be drinking alcohol to numb yourself, which might worsen the inclination towards alcoholism.

Or maybe you're not sleeping enough, and that could make you vulnerable to injuries or illnesses. For all these reasons, you need to check in with your doctor if you think you have a complicated case of grief. With the right medicine and the right psychological help, you'll soon feel a lot better. Statistics tell us that newly bereaved people are going to the doctor more often than those who are not bereaved. We used to assume that this meant that the loss of a loved one caused the survivor to get ill. We now assume that increased visits to a physician typically occur for the following reasons:

➢ Prior to death, the survivor had been busy caring for the ill patient and had little time to go to the doctor for himself or herself.

➢ The survivor now understands how critical it is to get proper medical care.

And you're not going to die of a broken heart. Family support and social support minimize grief responses. The more involvement you have with family members and the more social connections you have, the better your grief would be. Yet even those who are bereaved and have no help can survive and ultimately live well.

Often one of the partners joins another in death. It's not that one death hastens the other. There are cases in which a couple consists of two very elderly people and, statistically speaking, the elderly die. There are cases in which both partners have similar unhealthy habits — perhaps smoking, overeating, or not taking their prescribed medicines. These practices tend to promote death. According to all the most recent scholarly research, there is no elevated mortality risk for the bereaved.

If you come across an old study that "proves" that there is, just ignore it. If all the widows died immediately after their husbands died, we would not see 12 million widows in the United States. Nor will we have a crowd of bereaved parents filling the meeting rooms, seminars, and blogs with their scary stories.

Strange Stuff Is Happening

Often, during this challenging period of bereavement, you can feel like your brain is playing tricks on you. Do you have Visitation Dreams? Visitation dreams sound like the visits of your loved one. Within the first months after your death, your dreams could be sick, or whatever it was that caused death. Later, however, dreams typically represent a lighter and happier time.

In your dream, you will see your beloved, and he will be alive. Maybe he'll be a lot younger than when he died, or maybe he'll be the way he was. Often such dreams have a vivid color and show a lot of action. Many bereaved people are looking forward to the night so that they can experience the dream of a visit. In certain cultures, visitation dreamers claim that they are in contact with the spirit of the dead. For most

Americans, though, these visions help to preserve their bond with the dead. Dreams are evidence that the relationship persists, even after death.

You have flashbulb memories?

Flashbulb memory is a memory of a single significant event that is as vivid as if it were images of your brain. You'll still recall the specifics of those events. You may know exactly where you were and what you were doing when you learned about the 9/11 terrorist attacks. If you're older, you might know where you were when MLK was assassinated. And now, you've probably got flashbulb memories of your death or reaction to it. You're not going to have to scan the memory for death knowledge because the memories are as transparent as snapshots.

Are you going to have hallucinations?

Do you think you're hearing the footsteps of your loved one? Can you smell the aftershave lotion? Can you hear that your dead child is calling your name? Can you hear the voice of your mother? If you're so desperate to hear your dead husband's car pull into the driveway, you're probably going to hear it one sad day. It's natural to sometimes "forget" that the dead person is permanently gone. Hallucination helps to sustain the illusion that your loved one is nearby. You need that feeling a few days.

Ghost accounts and successful sessions can be due to the urgent need to be close to the deceased. It's nothing to think about.

Are you losing you memory of the death?

Any of your conduct is motivated by habit. You're so used to engaging with the person who's gone that sometimes you're going to continue your interactive behaviors. The widower, alone in his house, when he hears the phone ringing, yells, "I have it, honey." He literally repeats decades of habit. Even, the widow, who misplaced the dinner table for two, repeats decades of habit. According to reports, for the first few months after the death of a partner, a surviving spouse frequently feels embarrassed when she learns that she's looking for him in a crowd. This habit, too, is gone.

Are you going to cry?

Tears are soothing. They are a sign of courage and a testament of lost love. Know, only influential people dare to love deeply. Interestingly, emotional tears remove chemicals that build up in times of tension. Animals create tears that lubricate their eyes, but it is only humans that create emotional tears that extract harmful substances. That's right — the tears are helping the body. Crying decreases the amount of manganese in the body, which is a mineral that influences mood and is present in a high concentration of tears.

Researchers concluded that as tears remove chemicals built up by the body during stress, stress levels are reduced. It has been shown that the repression of tears raises stress levels. So, please grant yourself permission to cry. Keep a box of tissues in every room of your home and in your car, too. Tears in front of others, or in any public location, can easily trigger nurturing. When you need a hug, note that crying is an important way of communication. Bereaved families are bonded when they all weep together. Men are often accused of being cruel because they usually cry less than women do.

Please understand that men and women express their hurts in different ways. Women are talking and weeping. Men are more likely to take action. They could hit a wall or hit a ball. But when they get around to crying, they insist they feel better. Maimonides, a great medieval philosopher, said, "Those who grieve find comfort in weeping and in arousing their sorrow until the body is too tired to bear the inner emotions."

You will gain some power over your tears during the middle process over bereavement. You can find it helpful to define a specific place and time for crying. For example, understanding that you're going to weep after dinner in the living room will help you hold on to your tears on a working day. Some people are permitted to weep on the weekend, but not during the week. Others just scream in the bathroom, when no one can hear, or only in the car, when they're home.

In ancient Rome, the mourners filled small, decorative glass bottles with their tears and then put the bottles in the tombs to bury the dead. This was their way of showing gratitude and showing love to others. In fact, it was said that the most influential people had been buried with the most tear bottles.

Psalm 56:8 in the Old Testament of the Bible, shows that God takes note of our tears and keeps a record of our pain and suffering. David prays, saying, "Put thou my tears in Thy bottle; are they not in Thy Book?" The concept of gathering tears is obvious here, and what the bottle alluded to is probably a bottle of water.

In the Victorian era, fancy tear bottles were lined up in mourners' houses. During the time of solemnity, the bottles were considered acceptable decorations. Supposedly, as the liquid evaporated in the bottles, it was time to avoid mourning. Some of the U.S. Civil War stories mention the wives who cried in tear bottles and then saved all the bottles before their husbands came home from battle.

You may enjoy collecting tear bottles or having one or two bottles on your bedside or on a shelf. If you want to fill them with tears, that's all right, but it's not important. You may just want to keep them in your house as beautiful works of art, and every time you look at your tear bottles, you'll be reminded that weeping is good for you, and weeping is expected.

Are you going through stress?

We recognize that tension, which used to be called nervousness, happens during and after stressful experiences. The death of a loved one is a very painful occurrence. We also know that if stress lasts for too long, the immune system can be compromised. It's not a positive thing to be constantly depressed. So, to make your bereavement easier and to make sure that you are not vulnerable to infection due to a weakened immune system, you must break the stress loop in your body. You can do this by using medications and/or you can do this by using all the established methods of minimizing stress. These approaches shall include:

- Rest

- Music

- Practicing Yoga

- Reading and Writing Poetry

- Maintaining healthy Friendship

- Therapy

- Going on a Vacation

- Exercise

- Marveling at the sun

HELPING YOURSELF THROUGH THE PROCESS OF GRIEF

What would you do to make you feel better?

You need to take action often. When you do anything to ease your feelings and give yourself a sense of accomplishment, you make your path through bereavement. Here are some activities — and some habits that you should do — that are therapeutic to you during your bereavement.

Work is Therapeutic

If you're lucky enough to have a career, go back to it even if it's on a part-time basis. The structure of getting up and out, the duty to welcome fellow staff, and the need to be together for the necessary number of hours is good for you. If you don't have a job, it's time for you to volunteer at an animal shelter, a local daycare center, or a gift shop in the hospital.

Socialising Is Therapeutic

It's critical that you are among the people. Lack of interaction with friends and colleagues is an indicator of bereavement difficulties. There are potentially people who don't want to mess with your life at this time and who are purposely staying away. If you feel alone, then it's a good idea to get in contact with the people who are being too polite. Set up a date for lunch, a weekend stroll, or a shopping trip. Adopt a new social agenda and say "yes" if you're invited.

Organization Is Therapeutic

When life threatens to overwhelm you, it feels good to have power over something — even if it's just a space, a desk drawer, a closet, or a shelf. Get back under control by organizing one part of your home at a time. This is a good chance to find out what to do with your loved one's things. Many people are helped by getting all the loved ones' possessions, items, and clothes into one room. The rest of the house becomes easier to navigate, and that one special area is your "work in progress." Over the next few weeks or months, you will consolidate items in that area, give away what others will appreciate, and eventually have all your personal belongings in some boxes, drawers, or shelves.

When you need a feeling of closeness to your wife, you'll know where to go. Take the time to decide what you want to keep for yourself when going through things. It's a good idea to select some transitional objects. The adult form of a safety blanket is a transitional product. It's something that gives you that old, cozy, soothing feeling. Choose something that belongs to, or represents, your loved one.

Food is Therapeutic

Nourish your body well, and it's going to be good for you. Use your mealtime as a social gathering and invite your neighbors and acquaintances to join you. Plan ahead so that you'll have a business to eat. Get along with others for a Sunday breakfast, a Wednesday dinner, or a mid-week lunch at a restaurant.

Take the time to check out unique recipes online or in cookbooks. Find a recipe that looks attractive, practice it, and then master it. This will become your signature dish that the guests are looking forward to. Do you have any homeless people in your town? Offer them a little something to eat.

My neighbor Hal was too sad to eat after his wife died. When some of us in the street noticed his weight loss, we decided to take turns stopping at dinner time and bring some treats with us. He was too depressed to get out of his bed. Then, after a few weeks, Hal felt well enough to accept invitations to dinner. He may be found at one or the other of the neighbors' homes for a few nights each week. At this time, the son of one of the neighbors had a high school assignment that needed him to teach an adult something. He wanted to show Hal how to prepare soup. What a jackass! And Hal is inviting us over for food these days. Food therapy has supported him during bereavement.

Planting is Therapeutic

Using a calendar to make arrangements for you. Project when you're going to be different. Plan when you buy a new outfit for yourself. Intend to learn how to knit and decide when to go to the yarn store. Plan to go fishing and call a friend who likes to fish. Or, learn how to frame your favorite photo and prepare when you walk into a craft shop or an art supplies store. Plan to fix something in your house and plan to go to the Home Depot or Lowe's or the nearest hardware store. Planning your future will allow you to achieve the future.

Religion is Therapeutic

Therapy Rituals help the bereaved. Investigate what your religion has to give you. What does a newly bereaved person recommend to do? Try it, and if you're trying to find solace, go ahead. If you think it's a waste of time, or if it makes you too angry, talk to your clergy and see what else you can do to better yourself in the name of faith. Look for the clergy; they are there to support you in your sorrow, even though you are not a member of their congregation or, in many cases, of their religion.

There are also useful facets of faith to the bereaved. There is the union of voices in the song, the prayer, the person in authority telling you that you will be supported, the regularity of the time of the meeting, the social aspect of service, and the soothing words in religious readings. A believer is going to find solace in faith.

After death, some believers become non-believers. If you belong to the latter group, please think about attending services anyway. You might have some fun in the process, even though you're mad at God. You may find yourself caught up in a conversation with a clergyman who can help you find your way.

Writing Is Therapeutic

Putting your thoughts and emotions into words is going to help you. A friend says that daily writing helped her get through the first awful year after her son was killed. She remembers, "I'd just write and weep and write and weep. It was my therapy." There are several valuable writing activities, such as:

- Write about the last few days of your loved one's life, and then write about the day of death.

Say it all. Remember all the information and write them down.

Art is Therapeutic

If you're interested in presenting yourself artistically, you're in good company. Some mourners do not speak in words but convey their emotions in imaginative ways by drawing, sculpting, writing poetry, writing songs, essays, plays, and more. You don't need to be an experienced artist or poet. You just need to sit down and share your feelings. Novices and professional artists find creative expression during bereavement therapy.

Learning is Therapeutic

Good self-esteem helps you adapt to your new lifestyle, a lifestyle that requires an empty chair. The best way to improve self-esteem is to be good at doing things. There are adult, continuing education courses in your local high school, your local college, and the library, too. Learn to get a new skill. There is a reciprocal relationship between integrity and successful adaptation to the loss of a loved one. Take a one-day class or a full-time class. Take part in a one-hour lecture or a summer school session. Learn how to do a magic trick or how to cultivate orchids.

Know, know, learn, learn. Is there something you're really interested in? It's time to explore the interest. Will you like to learn to juggle? Will you like to learn how to play mah-jongg? How about a beekeeping course? Maybe you've always wanted to know more about politics, and you'd like to have a class in current affairs. You may have always wanted to know how to use your digital camera. You should take a course in photography. Learn to dance the country or learn to play the piano. Learn how to become a real estate appraiser or learn how to bake a cake. Learning is becoming you.

Reading is Therapeutic

At first, you will find it too difficult to focus on a long novel, and it would be best to read only short pamphlets, magazine posts, and then selected chapters. There are a plethora of books on sorrow, death, and overcoming loss.

Please don't restrict your reading to bereavement books, please. Reading can be a wonderful escape to other lands and other ages. Novels will intrigue you and take your mind away from your sorrow. Memoirs will involve you in the life of someone else. Mysteries can force you to use your brain to think of someone else's problem, not you — a welcome relief.

Sweet Moments

Pay attention to those moments when you're not calm. What the heck are you doing in those moments? Keep a list of things you do that offer you solace, written or emotional. If an unhappy moment is coming up, just check your list, and you'll know how to get back to your sweet moment. Here's a collection of lists from some of my clients that were asked to complete the sentence, "I feel very good when I do…"

- Talk on the phone with my sister
- Take the dog for a long stroll.
- Take a peek at the pictures of our last holiday.
- Play games online.
- Listen to music.
- Take a bubble bath.
- Pray.
- Take a look at the sunrise
- Listen to a reassuring CD.
- Get up on work-related reading.

- Watch any of the sitcoms.

- Go to a movie

- Focus on my scrapbook.

- Have your manicure.

- Visit your grandchildren.

- Clean, clean and clean — the garage, the basement, everything.

- Overtime jobs and search for further work assignments.

- Take a long drive away.

- Cuddling up with some of his clothing.

- Hang out with your parents. They're reminding me of him.

- Look at the exquisite art of a museum or gallery.

- Visit the park; take a stroll.

LIVING THROUGH GRIEF: GETTING OUTSIDE ASSISTANCE

You're not alone here. Support is available now. You may decide to turn to your neighbor, your rabbi, your coach, or your counselor — or your minister, your mother, your psychotherapist, or your librarian. Whoever you want is going to have suggestions. Then it's up to you to decide which advice you're going to pursue. This chapter is going to get you started. It gives an overview of all the ways in which you can get bereavement support.

Bereavement Groups

Most adults who are widowed or lose a parent or loved one need only help from a friend or family member. Within a year or two, they're going back to the way they were before death, and they're going to be able to get through their day without a problem. Most people are resilient; they experience extreme transitory depression after death, and then get over it.

Bereavement groups may still be helpful, however, even to those who heal by themselves. If you're still feel happier when you're around like-minded people, a group is going to be of use to you. Or, if you're lonely and want to be a friend, this is a good way to initiate social interactions.

If you're not a talker and you're not one to express your thoughts, you might not appreciate a tell-all support group, but you may benefit from a less invasive bereavement group. It is the personality of the leader of the party that typically dictates whether or not the agenda requires uncovering your soul. Some leaders are low-key and do not promote the exchange of feelings unless you, the bereaved, initiate it. My recommendation is to go to a meeting and then determine whether to satisfy your needs. You're going to know whether you're happy there or not.

Mutual support helps because people who have similar experiences may give advice to each other. They know what's working and what's not working. They're on the front lines. During your bereavement, you can become ultra-conscious of all those people who appreciate a relationship you no longer have. If your spouse is gone, you will see married couples wherever you are. When your parent died, you appear to be the only one without your mom or dad. If your child died, you might conclude that no one else has ever had such a tragic loss. But, luckily, everybody in your bereavement party is just like you. Members of your mourning party act as your role models. They're living evidence that you can survive this trauma. They give visible proof that life goes on.

Only someone who has been through what you're going through will give you valuable advice on daily circumstances. There are important pieces of information best given by the members of your bereavement support group

If you've become a widow and don't know a lot of other widows, you're going to profit from talking to someone who has recently lost a friend. Members of your widow's community will tell you whether, why, and when they removed their wedding bands or switched their rings to the other side. They're going to share advice on dealing with the in-laws and dealing with the clothing closet. They know about Social Security, and they know that they're sitting alone in a restaurant.

People tell me that their support group members are supporting them in ways I have never been able to. If you have lost a child, you will benefit from meeting other parents in the same circumstances. Losing a child causes immeasurable sorrow and pain, no matter the age of that child. Grieving parents sometimes feel like their mates become strangers because they can not grasp the depths of their sorrow. When the mourning parents join the bereaved-parent support group, they believe the strangers in the group becoming friends. Those are the people who can understand; they've been there. They know about removing babies from the nursery and removing toys from the toy cabinet. They even hear about the sensitive handling of siblings and grandparents.

Parents who have lost a child are especially thankful to other parents who are helping them to reconnect with the outside world — the world beyond serious grief. For example, the answer to the question that parents were afraid of—"How many children do you have? "— is frequently addressed in bereaved-parent sessions. Parents report that at the beginning of the bereavement, if a well-meaning friend should ask that question, it might cause hysterics or, as Betty recalled, "I just ran away, jumped into my car, and headed for home and bed." Parents need each other and learn from each other.

In *Recovering from the Loss of a Child,*, Katherine Fair Patriot writes, "Parents want to talk. They need someone to listen to the crying of their soul." She also said, "The shock impact of a child's death leaves parents with one of the cruelest of all emotions—the total sense of powerlessness." Parents believe that they will protect their child. Those parents whose child died are forced to accept that they are not in charge and that their child has succumbed even though they have done their best.

Group Benefits

You can find that your group offers you the opportunity to speak about your loved one in a way that brings him or her back to life for you during the meetings. This makes you face the truth of your loss more quickly. After a while, at your own rate, you will cause the picture of your beloved to become a reassuring memory. Inside your party, you will remember the good times and the poor, go through the specifics of your death, and then use the input of the members of the group to prepare your future.

A bereavement community offers you a place to address topics that your friends and family might not be involved in. Like you, the others who are bereaved think about the injustice of life.

- Do you get angry when you see people walking in the street who are older than your loved one?
- Do you get angry when you see people of bad character who are still alive?

The randomness of the disease is most noticeable when you visit a hospital and see extreme suffering, and then visit a jail where many prisoners are in great health and can live their entire lifetime. Life may be unfair. We don't always get what we deserve. Sometimes good people die young. Calamities often hit at random. This is well known by the community members.

In a good bereavement party, you are free to share your feelings without fear of criticism. Friends and family, on the other hand, want you to sprint quickly through bereavement and return to your old self. Since they mean well, and it hurts them to see you so depressed, they prefer to give unsolicited support and recommend a quick recovery. They just don't get it — you're going to heal, but at your own pace. This has always been an established reality. The Old Testament includes a verse that is beneficial and wise in times of sorrow, regardless of your faith or lack thereof:

To every thing there is a season, And a time to every purpose under the heaven: A time to be born, and a time to die; A time to plant, and a time to pluck up that which is planted; A time to kill, and a time to heal; A time to break down, and a time to build up; A time to weep, and a time to laugh; A time to mourn, and a time to dance; A time to cast away stones, and a time to gather stones together; A time to embrace, and a time to refrain from embracing; A time to get, and a time to lose; A time to keep, and a time to cast away; A time to rend, and a time to sew; A time to keep silence, and a

time to speak; A time to love, and a time to hate; A time of war, and a time of peace.

—ECCLESIASTES 3:1–8

Bereavement groups have been of importance for decades. Beginning in the twelfth century, Jewish mourners recited a popular prayer called the Kaddish. From the day of burial, which lasted eleven months after the death of a parent, religious Jewish mourners, along with other members of their congregation, assemble once or twice a day to sing the prescribed words.

This may sound burdensome, but the practice of Kaddish is successful for the following reasons:

• *Grief responses shall be normalized.* If people in your circle are going through just what you're going through, you begin to believe that your emotions and emotions are right.

• *Display of emotion is encouraged.* You're supposed to sing words with passion, and they're especially strong words. It's a passionate recitation.

• *Trust is encouraged.* Prayer itself is a public praise of God, spoken only at a time when life has been taken, and faith can fade.

• *Quiet assistance is given.* Everyone in the church understands that you are there to mourn the loved one and respect your condition. There is a particular time during the religious service where mourners are asked to stand up and say Kaddish. Saying Kaddish drags a person out of the house and interrupts his or her isolation at a time when he or she may be tempted to hide under the shelter for days at a time. This tradition offers a framework on a day that could easily become disorganized and disrupted. The first mourners to say that Kaddish may have unintentionally set up the world's first bereavement support group.

The best part of the support group is that it's the best place to get help. If someone has been bereaved more recently than you join your party, you can leave your dependent state for a moment and uncover your strengths. It's a positive thing for you and the new member of the party.

The Advantages and Disadvantages of Bereavement Counselors

Sensitive therapeutic assistance is often warranted during bereavement, but grievance-focused counseling is needed only for the few mourners who develop complicated grievances. Complicated grief, as discussed earlier, is severe and excessive grieving that does not give up.

Usually, if there is a need for bereavement counseling, it will be reasonable to intervene several months after the death, not immediately after death. Often counselors insist that if a loved one has died, you need their services. A bereavement counselor may want to meet with you to help you find your way through the bereavement process.

Trust me, you know how to grieve, you don't need a teacher. Standard reactions do not need to be studied. If bereavement therapy is to be effective, it is best given several months to one year after death. It's time for the mourners to know if they still have death problems. And that's definitely when the mourners know whether they have a complex grief. Most of the people, though, would feel great by then. Please contact a bereavement counselor if you have a difficult case of grief.

I do not recommend bereavement advice immediately after death. If well-meaning counselors rush to school after a student dies or rush to a shooting scene, they can do more harm than good. For many people, learning about death soon after it happens breaks the normal numbness period that is supposed to be protective. Such talk could increase sadness. It is easier to allow sorrow to follow its natural pace and gradually emerge and then gradually dissipate.

HELPING CHILDREN COPE WITH GRIEF

Educator and author Eda LeShan notes, "A child can live through anything, so long as he or she is told the truth and is allowed to share with loved ones the natural feelings people have when they are suffering." But, for most of us, facing the painful reality of death with a child seems an unbearable challenge. Our own fears of death and ignorance of death, so common in our culture, make it incredibly difficult to face death honestly and specifically with children. Thus, because of our own inhibitions, we sometimes deprive children of the chance to begin to grapple with their loss and their ideas of death.

Few families are discussing death as part of their children's educational and social agenda. Parents like to believe that death does not happen, and who can blame us? All parents want to shield their offspring from pain, grief, and fear. It's the desire to protect the sends parents to the pet shop to replace the dead goldfish they had flared away when their child was in school. Imagine for a moment that the child had come home from school to see their pet is dead. Yes, the child will be angry. Yes, the infant is going to weep. And yeah, the child's going to get over it fast.

The child will have evidence that he or she might face death, cry in grief, and then recover. It's not a bad lesson to remember. The luckiest children are those whose first human death encounters are people they did not count on. A distant relative, a friend's parent, or a former neighbor, are not child-critical relationships. It's not that these deaths are unimportant. Rather, it is easier to witness death from a distance than it is for a child to mourn the loss of a near relative. Don't shelter your children; let them know about these deaths. Your children will know that they can live with death, and they'll still be all right. This provides a blueprint for good coping with subsequent deaths

Our attitudes towards children also prohibit us from sharing with them freely and honestly. Since we have trouble recognizing and embracing death, we sometimes persuade ourselves that death is beyond children's grasp. On the one hand, we seem to deny that children sense, possibly pain, human beings, and, on the other hand, we imagine that they are too undeveloped to experience true sorrow. In the other side, we fear how profoundly children will suffer from loss, and we want to spare or shield them from enduring grief.

Similarly, we do not want to scare or overwhelm them with our tears. They may be afraid of crying, but they can heal more quickly if they say the truth. Even if the details of death are not shared, children invariably know the truth, or at least experience trouble. They suffer all the more in isolation.

The apparent shortcomings of children further prevent us from facing death with them. We may avoid trying to communicate seriously with them since they are characteristically unable to communicate in an adult way. We may become irritated with them for their inability to communicate their feelings, or we may even come to assume that there is none when feelings remain unexpressed. Of course, restricted child vocabulary and often inhibited reactions to emotions may interfere with intimate discussions. Some adolescents, however, are so disarmingly frank about their feelings that they cause anxiety in adults who are not as transparent. When children are able to convey deep emotions, it indicates that they are emotionally balanced.

While children have many of the same emotions that adults have, their outward appearance is much more confused or defensive. Children's protective reactions to loss may be frustrating or anxiety-producing to adults, who then shy away from expressing their own feelings. Children can respond defensively when faced with the fact of death. For example, they might say things like "Bang, bang, you're dead" or "I don't love him anyway," or they might laugh anxiously. At first, they may change the subject, run away to play, show resentment that their activities are suddenly reduced, or seem to have no specific reaction to the news of death. Adults can support a child with grief and death by giving less weight to the child's attitude and by continuing to be transparent, frank, and kind, regardless of the child's behaviour. Unfortunately, in conditions of tension, sympathy between parents and children is frequently interrupted.

When death happens, children should be told the truth immediately in a caring, normal way, ideally by a parent or someone close to them. The words and explanations of death need to be simple, direct, and honest. We should share our own convictions, our concerns, and our own questions. By ignoring problems and emotions, we're going to fail our children. Euphemisms, such as saying that a dead loved one "goes away on holiday," clouds and negates reality. Likewise, sending children away from the family or the circumstance of grief or denying their grief shows contempt for their feelings, and denies them their rightful grief. Being sent away will seem like a cruel punishment to a child, and it will increase the already growing sense of anguish.

Grief is difficult for children since the fear of separation from their parents is so prevalent. Loss can seem to threaten the very life of a child. Absence of a parent can cause extreme distress in young children, and without anyone to fulfill their physical and emotional needs, their lives seem to be in danger.

Therefore, children need to be told that they will not be left behind and that their needs will be met. When children grow older and become more independent in their abilities and relationships outside the family, the anxieties of separation decrease. Fear of separation is a matter for each, and every one of us before our freedom and individuality are clearly defined. While the symptoms of grief in children may be less noticeable than in adults, children are grieving.

Their grievance reactions are complicated by their sometimes unconscious attempts to conceal feelings and their protective acts. Children may respond defensively to news of death through denial, drowsiness, brazenness, or even jokes, all of which may dismay or anger the adults around them. Children will cling to daydreams that deny reality. The less they understand, the more likely they are to be apprehensive and scared.

They may be afraid that another loved one will die, and they may literally cling to that other person, or they may fear their own death.

Their grief can be sporadic or short-lived. A significant distinction between mourning parents and mourning children is that children typically do not feel depressed for long periods of time. Children may not be able to verbally share their reactions to death. Often children can be able to express themselves more easily by telling a story or drawing an illustration of their experiences. Sharing their feelings through stories or drawings may be a meaningful way for angry or mourning children to release their emotions. We should always be mindful that children will feel when adults do not want them to express their feelings. When children are closed down in this way, it also results in a harmful habit of swallowing their emotions to appease others.

Important, too, when children do not disclose their emotions, it is their concern for those around them. Sometimes a child is unable to communicate what he or she feels to his or her parents, because the parents, too, maybe upset by something that has happened, and the child feels defensive of them; he or she does not want to cause them any more distress and unhappiness. If parents are able to face their own emotions freely, the child will be more readily opened up with his own emotions and uncertainty.

Death reactions vary depending on the age of the child or the stage of growth. Psychologist Maria Nagy states the following developmental variations in the responses of children to death. Around three to five years of age, children prefer to see death as anything like sleep or a journey from which one can wake up or return. The permanence of death has not yet been understood. Around five to nine years of age, children grasp the fact of death, but they have trouble in believing that they or their loved ones will die. At nine or ten years of age, children understand the inevitable essence of death. At the same time, they are more interested about its biological aspects and are mindful of the social consequences of death and loss for survivors. Teenagers may revert to earlier concepts of death, but they are generally concerned, as do adults, with the quest for the meaning of death.

Children have the most difficult time embracing death when they have had the least training for loss and death. It's hard for us to prepare for the unexpected loss of a loved one. However, we should begin to prepare the child for death itself long before it has to face it. Instead of avoiding the topic of death with youngsters, the awareness of death as a regular fact is a kind of planning. Most children see death early in life, whether it's a dead insect, duck, squirrel, or a personal pet. Usually less charged, these deaths provide an opportunity for children and adults to discuss together the problems that are bound to occur for any child regarding death, whether or not the child verbalizes them.

The question of a child may be: what is death? Why are we dying? Am I going to die? Are you going to die? What's going to happen after death? When ideas are not truly articulated to them, children appear to scare themselves and imagine the worst. Exploring these problems before a significant loss happens not only helps the child examine death, it also allows parents an opportunity to confront tough issues without having to deal with fear and sorrow at the same time. However, parents may need to build their own understanding of death in order to be able to support the infant.

Most significantly, parents can help a child embrace death by treating death as a natural reality, recognizing and spontaneously reflecting on death. If the opportunity occurs, parents and children can bury a dead animal together. This could lead the child to explore various definitions of death.

As a boy, my failed attempts to dig a dead canary long after I buried it contributed to my admission that death was permanent.

Death management for children may rely on whether death is abrupt or follows a chronic illness. Kids, like adults, experience shock and denial when they first hear a loss. Advance planning decreases the sense of shock and makes it easier for them to cope with the loss. Children should not be sheltered from the death process of a loved one. Shielding children from dying denies them the ability to stay in touch with the dying loved one and intensifies the shock of death. Too many of my clients were still experiencing as adults the pain of sudden, unprepared death of a loved parent or grandparent because they were excessively shielded from illness and death as children.

Sharing the dying process can be a rare and satisfying experience for both of us. A caring child will provide a great deal of comfort to the person who is dying. Having a chance to share with a dying loved one often allows children to learn about death in a normal way; they can share their thoughts with a loved one, and otherwise, unfinished business can be done before death happens. Even if children may appear to doubt that a loved one is dying, or that they have trouble in developing a sense of death, when the reality is shared, they have a better chance of truly mourning and embracing loss. There could be severe consequences if we protect children from death. Children are profoundly influenced by silence, as well as by avoidance, denial, and death fiction. Death can terrorize excessively shielded children.

Children's sorrow can easily be inhibited. Often kids feel embarrassed to weep. They are often discouraged by wrong adults who urge them to "Be brave" or "Be a little guy" or "Be a sweet, quiet person" or "Don't be a cribaby." Children often react obediently to these injunctions and stifle their own sorrow at their cost. Like I said earlier, grief is a learned action. Adults may help and assist a child to grieve entirely, or adults may restrict the child's ability to grieve through their words or injunctions and by the actions they give the child to emulate. Both words and acts inform children about grief, as well as other life experiences.

Children would be more able to recognize the finality of death after they have attended the funeral or visited the graveyard. The usual explanation why children are likely to be afraid at a funeral is that they will witness adults being out of control. It could be the first time a child has ever seen a mom, or any adult, crying. If a child has always relied on adults in the family to be strong and support her when she's in a jam, imagine how terrified she would be when she's witnessing the death of a loved one and all her other loved ones are inaccessible to her because they're wailing and crying. I recommend that a close friend or family member be assigned to stay with a child during the funeral service.

Listen to Your Children

The more you talk about death, the more likely you are to explain situations and clear up myths. Pay close attention to everything that your children say after they've experienced or are going through a loss.

Have Conversations with your Children

Children will need proof that disease does not necessarily cause death. We all get sick, and then we recover; health is a normal condition. It's the odd exception who succumbs to the disease. Bereaved children, like some bereaved adults, often assume they have the same symptoms as the deceased. Please demonstrate to the child that it is possible to have the same symptoms and to live a healthy and long life. Say the reality about that. Use the word dead, man. This is the reality, and it prevents the child from thinking that the individual is coming back soon. It allows the child to adapt to the finality of the case. Saying that the deceased is in deep sleep can create difficulties in the future. To claim that the deceased is away on a long journey will create separation difficulties. You don't want to foster the hope that the individual is coming back. You do want to foster the expectation that the child will be excited about life again.

Understand Your Children

Some children do not seem to worry about the death of a loved one. They don't cry, they don't act, they don't seem sad. Some children behave as if nothing odd has happened. This indifference is typically a child's way of creating the confidence to mourn. It is the mental preparation that is required before mourning can begin.

Young children are seeking out different ways to relate to a loved one who has died. They could speak to him, research his pictures, keep special things that belonged to him, and sometimes dream about him. Many children believe that a dead person, particularly if he is a father, is watching them.

Like I said earlier, when a parent dies, make sure that no one tells the child that he or she is now the man or woman in the home. It is tragic that a parent has been taken away from the child; do not exacerbate the tragedy by taking away the child's childhood, too. It's childhood that makes it possible for the infant to be dependent and to get treatment and cuddling.

Researchers reassure us that children in stable families are recovering well and are not overwhelmed by their loss. In a retrospective study of college women who had lost their parents years earlier, researchers found that while women thought that their lives had changed since their death, none of them indicated that their lives were especially troubled or troubled.

The best predictors of a child's recovery from grief are relationships with family members and school mates. If the relationship is good, the consequence of the sorrow is intense. Of course, if you're a surviving parent, you need to do what you can to continue parenting. The child has lost one of the parents to death. You wouldn't want to make it worse.

NOVEL FORMS OF APPROACH HEALING

Throughout your grief, please mourn the way you need to mourn, the way that is comforting to you. You will soon be redirecting your life to the future. Your appetite and your sleep are coming back. Your vitality is coming back. Your capacity to operate all day long will resurface.

The Tapping Cure

In addition to the helpful instructions in the preceding pages, there are two advanced methods that are especially useful to bereaved people: tapping and visualization.

The tapping cure is a self-help process, very similar to acupressure. It does not use drugs and does not use talk therapy. It needs you to press, with your fingertips, specific points of your body while at the same time talking about what is bothering you. Tapping will help to remove the feelings of distress. You should get rid of the negative emotions that you associate with those thoughts. Tapping distinguishes a painful feeling from a particular thought. So, you may still have your feelings, but they're not going to make you feel so bad. Really, they're not going to make you feel bad at all.

I suggest that you try the process. You've got nothing to lose but a few minutes and all to win. I'd like you to use four fingers on either hand to tap the following spots to launch the tapping remedy.

1. *Below your eye,* the bone. Either eye is all right. This is a very useful tapping spot for bereavement.

2. *The junction between your nose and your inner eyebrow.* Try tapping with one or two fingers on that spot.

3. *Your collarbone.* Use both fingertips on your hands to tap on either side of your collarbone.

While there are several other tapping spots on your hands and face, the three spots I've just introduced are typically the most powerful when it comes to bereavement issues. Now try this: tap your eyebrow spot, under the eye spot, the collarbone, your side, and then the spot on the top of your palm.

The second half of this healing practice is to find out what to say while taping. Repeat one sentence while tapping at each location. You repeat your sentence as you pass from spot to spot. Think of a few words or a phrase to formulate your sentence, one that explains your worst feelings.

Among the sentences chosen by some of my bereaved clients are the following:

- I am so lonely.

- The best friend of mine is gone.

- The chair is still empty.

- I hate to sleep alone in our king-size bed.

- I 'm feeling a hole in my middle.

Please write down your sentence. Your sentence should define the situation that is most stressful for you, the situation that is disrupting your life today. If nothing is so distressing to you today, then you don't need a tapping remedy today.

If you're in trouble, write your sentence right now. Then tap the following two words at the beginning of your sentence: "Even though." Fine. Now add the following words to the end of your sentence: "I can deal with it." So, if your original sentence was "I am miserable because I miss my beloved very, very much," your full sentence will now be, "Even though I am miserable because I miss my beloved very, very much I can deal with it."

Here are some other possibilities for finishing the sentence:

- I 'm going to be over it soon.

- I 'm looking forward not backward

- I've got a decent life ahead of me.

- I'll be all right shortly.

- I should behave like this isn't a big deal.

- I'm embracing myself.

- I love myself, man.

- I'm really lovable.

Say these:

- Even though the chair is still empty, I embrace myself.

- Even though I'm so lonely, I'm going to be fine really soon.

- Even though I miss my wife, I know that I'm a lover.

- Even though I'm sad right now, I can always do what needs to be done.

- Even though I feel like my life is over, I know I'm going to recover soon.

- Even though I'm nervous, I embrace myself.

- Even though I'm mad at him for dying, I love myself.

- Even though he left me in a bad time, I'm going to get back to myself.

- Even though life is too unfair, I embrace myself.

- Even though I've buried my baby, I'm still going to live

Looking down at the paper you've written your completed sentence, you should start clicking. Please, tap each time you say your sentence. Then stop, take a deep breath and see how you feel. You'll actually feel a lot better and a lot less frustrated. You might want to repeat the tap sequence a couple of times — after all, it takes less than a minute to do all the taps.

Pay attention to yourself and your emotions as you tap and decide if one or two of the tapping spots are more successful than the others. Then determine if one or two of the spots seem to have no effect. Now you can configure your tapping protocol to suit your needs. You may want to get rid of one or two spots and focus on the others and go through your tapping routine again. You should feel a lot better by this time. Test yourself by thinking about your original scenario, and note your reaction to it. It doesn't bother you anymore, doesn't it? You've done a decent job.

You may use tapping to ease the effects of grief and to support you with other pressures and stressful emotions in your life. Feelings of abandonment, rage, treachery, isolation, and boredom react well to a tapping remedy.

Some people tap to start their day every morning. Others tap before bedtime. Some tap for a couple of consecutive days, and then they never need to tap again because they've mastered their situation. Some tap in anticipation of a tough time ahead — that is, right before a visit to those people or the anniversary of death.

You'll get the best results if you press at a moment when you're highly emotional and very distressed.

The Power of Visualization

The process of visualizing specific images, often referred to as directed images, is a self-help technique. It is a tool that helps you to use your mind to make you feel better and work at a more productive and successful level. You simply imagine a useful image in your head, and then your brain absorbs the image and integrates it into your life. This method helps you to enjoy a new thinking, a new mindset, or a new action.

Only sit back and relax. If you're more relaxed on a bed, that's all right. Don't think about falling asleep. As you read this section, you can decide to take breaks here and there by closing your eyes and imagining the scenes you're reading in your mind.

Find a quiet spot where you're not going to be interrupted. It's a place where there's no phone, no ipod — just you. This journey takes you down a road that helps you to feel good — very good — calm and happy, rested and relaxed.

You're going to love this wonderful mind / body experience.

1. *Take a deep breaths.* Allow your body to slow down. Nice. Feel the body relaxing. You're going to experience a lovely heavy feeling. It's a feeling of relief. You feel slowed down. Your hands and legs are so heavy and so silent. Your whole body is still.

2. *Slow down your mind.* Your mind is still there. Your emotions are going to slow down. Give yourself permission to feel comfortable in your mind. Nice. You read these words, and you feel very relaxed.

3. *Calm your nerves.* Imagine that you're going down the road. There's grass on both sides of you — see it in your head. And then you'll see some trees, some bushes and some lovely greenery.

4. *Pause to imagine.* Give yourself a few minutes to envision this scene.

5. You take the right path — this is where you should be — where you belong. Look up and see the blue sky — there's a cloud drifting around. See the glorious light. Feel the warmth of the sun, man. Listen carefully, and you could hear some birds, and there are other soothing sounds of nature, too.

6. Stop again, close your eyes and imagine this comforting scene with you in it for a few minutes.

7. Open your eyes and imagine again slowly. As you keep on walking, your burdens will be lifted. Please grant yourself permission to enjoy this walk. Yes, you will enjoy yourself. You have to enjoy yourself. It's a good idea for you to enjoy yourself. Stop for a moment and see the beauty all around you. Take a deep breath and enjoy the scent of nature.

Listen, listen to the sweet sounds of the outdoors. Notice the beauty of nature. Look at the colorful flowers. You're still going to have nature near you. You're still going to have the opportunity to be similar to beauty. And then you'll feel calm. You can imagine yourself on this road anytime you need to change your mood. This is a beautiful ride that you're on.

Enable yourself to feel protected, happy, relaxed and comfortable. You're well covered. You are comforted by the rays of the sun. The flowers are bringing joy to your heart. You're already walking. You enjoy yourself. Your body and mind are at rest.

You're getting calmer and calmer. Your mind's healing. Your mind restores your body. You can build this feeling of peace anytime you need to, simply by imagining your direction. The road is going to lead you to happiness. Continue to enjoy your walk and then pause whenever you like. Whenever you're ready, just keep reading and start walking around again. Stroll for as long as you want to.

Walk here, walk outside, smell the roses. Feel the calmness that surrounds you. You enjoy yourself. Note a lovely herb. There's a specific flower that's exceptional. The memory of this beautiful flower will linger in your mind. Whenever you see the flower in your mind, you will instantly come to this state of serenity, of calm, of silence.

Hang on the road as long as you want. Stay with your flower for as long as you want. If you want to stop reading this and close your eyes and see your flower, go ahead and do so. You feel safe and protected, relaxed and happy. Nice. Nice. Enjoy your feelings of comfort. Of comfort to you.

You deserve to have these positive feelings. You know now that you should feel fine. You should avoid the stresses of daily life. It's good for you. Look at the greens. There is a lovely tree. You are on a lovely stroll. Then, whenever you feel ready, you will begin to retrace your steps and go back to the beginning of the road.

When you are back at the beginning of the journey, slowly, at your own rate, you will begin to return your ordinary feelings back to your mind and return your ordinary feelings back to your body. Take your time, please. We've got a lot of time. You will continue to walk as long as you want. Then, when you're ready, you'll get back to your starting point on the road.

Enable your hands and feet to return to regularity. The heaviness of your body will steadily decrease. Take your time, you've got a lot of time.

You may want to stretch out, sit down, and go back to the normal. Nice. Nice. You've done a decent job.

Any positive feeling you've had on this journey will stay with you. Any good feeling you've had is a feeling you've developed. All the healthy, peaceful, restful feelings you encountered while reading this exercise came from inside you. These are your thoughts. You've got the ability to build them anytime you need them.

Read these words anytime you want to get back the wonderful feelings of peace and quiet. A beautiful feeling of serenity. Consolation.

Note that you return from your walk along the road with feelings of contentment. Whenever you want to replicate these feelings, just take a snapshot of the road in your mind and then see yourself walking in your mind.

Take a deep breath, please. Sit back and spread out. You're warning now, and you're able to restart your life. Lucky for you. You're just material. You will take care of your life with ease and pleasure. You've done a decent job on this road and with your flower.

HELPING OTHERS TO LIVE THROUGH GRIEF

It's hard for us survivors to confront loss and death. We feel overwhelmed and powerless when we learn about someone else's loss. One result of the denial of death in our culture is that we are always naive and unskilled in dealing with loss, be it our own or that of others. We may want to help, but we don't know how to do that. Having no idea what to do when we learn of death, many of us run away from helping the bereaved. There are, however, a variety of ways in which we can support others in their grief.

A grieving friend needs our friendship and support to go through and complete the process of grief. We need to reach out and take the lead in offering support. The most important thing we have to offer is our presence. It is much more important than our expertise or guidance, since the company of family and friends is the greatest source of encouragement and consolation. We can support our weeping friend best by sitting close, holding a hand, embracing, passing a tissue, crying together, listening, expressing our feelings. In other words, what the bereaved need most is our appreciation of their suffering and sorrow. And both of us must know that we can not erase that pain. In dealing with the loss, the bereaved are greatly energized. The presence of others tends to energize and refresh them. Often the mourners experience a decrease of morale as the visitors leave, as if they were other people who almost literally kept them up.

We always assume that there is a "right" way to behave, if only we knew what the right way was. Many of us fail to find the right words when a plain "I 'm sorry" is enough. While some words can provide consolation, there are few "right" words to cause sorrow. Being a loving presence and a good listener is more critical than any word we might say. Above all, the bereaved need caring people to stand by their suffering. This is exactly what help is all about. Not having to suffer on its own is also the best gift we can give the bereaved. Being alone is tougher. It's only when anxiety and anguish are overwhelming. Aloneness accentuates the desperation and emptiness of failure.

When supporting those who are grieving, we need to remember that people have different needs in different stages of grief. In the early period of shock, practical support is often most required, although emotional empathy does not yet reach the bereaved. However, emotional support is important during the traumatic time of grief.

If we don't know what to do for anyone else, a good rule of thumb is to ask ourselves, "What do I want to do for me in these circumstances?

"Another good rule is to feel — or ask specifically about — the needs of the mourner. For e.g., if the bereaved have to chat, we should respond by all means. If the other person needs to be silent, we should be silent, too, and not rush to fill the silence. And we must try to concentrate on sharing, not taking. The bereaved person wants a lot of support and rarely has a lot to give in return. If the mourner needs privacy, we're expected to stay away, so we're not putting any extra pressure on the mourner.

Practical help to those who grieve is often of great benefit. For example, considerate people who bring a casserole for dinner and leave are as appreciable as those who stick around for several hours. What is normally an easy task may be particularly challenging for the bereaved to manage. Answering the phone, monitoring phone messages or phone calls, getting groceries, making errands, cleaning dishes or home, listing who wrote or brought presents, and responding to notes of sympathy — all these are required activities that typically go beyond the ability of those in mourning.

There are also other daunting tasks involved in death that those in mourning can typically not completely manage on their own. The support of friends is a great comfort in coping with decisions such as the disposal of the body or the possessions of the deceased or in notifying those who need to be informed. The organization of people in the background, behind a mourning family, is a powerful aid in the time of loss.

We will help by not dragging them into the future. We need to keep a check on our own anxieties, which can cause us to challenge or offer advice. If decisions are to be taken, we can have to make a commitment to our best judgment. Whenever possible, it is better to make choices that leave room for a change of heart. We may also help a grieving friend delay an impulsive or irrational decision. The deceased also need a special friend to serve as a kind of spokesman or intermediary. This person may also serve as a trustee, as well as someone who may easily interfere with the mourning family.

Such an intermediary must be comfortable defending the bereaved, even though at times it means being impolite. When members of the family seem exhausted, the intermediary might screen phone calls or visitors or take responsibility for asking the guests to leave. It's a huge help to have a friend or friends who can give this unique kind of help. In order to be a genuinely supportive friend to the bereaved, we need to determine whether or not we can bear the suffering of the other. It is profoundly difficult to be a witness to deep mourning. It is tempting, when uncomfortable, because others are in the throes of sorrow, to cut them off, to urge them to stop weeping, to deny their suffering, or to try to hurry them through the excruciating phase of mourning. However, complete grief is appropriate and safe. Denying another chance to grieve completely is both a big intrusion and a denial.

If we can not bear the grief of the other individual, it is wrong for us to put ourselves through an ordeal. Instead, we can help from afar by phone or errands, or whatever needs to be done away with from the home of the bereaved.

If we are able to accept the strength of the feelings of loss and let go of our self-consciousness about doing the "right" stuff, there is something we can give to the bereaved. Tolerating the tears of another human is a really meaningful gift. So listen to me without judging. Often this means listening to the same ideas that have been repeated over and over. But that, too, is an essential gift. And if we're not sure what our job should be when the other one is crying, we can just get through the tissues!

People in pain are particularly responsive to those around them. Typically, they know who can stand their pain and who can't. Often it is those who have already suffered loss — those who know and understand suffering — who bring the most comfort. Mourners have a self-protective sense as to who can tolerate their suffering with them. Conversely, mourners who are unable to witness their pain will most certainly gravitate towards supporters who promote their denial.

Ways to help the bereaved vary, depending on the mourner. People who become disabled when mourning need support at every level. Others need to continue to work in order to attest to their ability to cope with losses. Both are natural responses, and we need to be responsive to the individual style of the grieving person. We should offer our help without taking over so much that the bereaved one feels disabled and without trying to save the other from feeling sad. We can also invite the bereaved to take part in social activities, invitations that they can freely accept or reject.

It's important to be sensitive about how long we've been in mourning while visiting people. In not knowing what to do, tourists often linger too long, looking for hints as to when to go. An individual in mourning, thankful for our presence, may not be comfortable asking us to leave.

Our recognition of the suffering is meaningful to the bereaved. That we care can be said in person, plainly and explicitly. We don't have to visit explicitly if we don't feel intimate or if we are uncomfortable facing grief.

You would appreciate a letter or phone call. A personal note, however brief, is always more consoling than a formal greeting card.

Other ways to express our condolences are by sending flowers or contributing to a charity in memory of the deceased. The most important gifts that people gave me when my brother died were the exchange of memories. Adding other anecdotes to my own memories has strengthened the wealth of my brother's memories. Each memory adds new dimensions or pictures of my brother, and let me know that he was as important to others as he was to me. Now, when I write a letter of condolence or visit the bereaved, I try to share my experience with the deceased, to offer the kind of vignette I loved myself. In other words, a meaningful letter of condolence may describe an event or characteristic of the deceased to make him or her live again in the eyes of the survivors.

It can also be useful to gather valuable mementos of the deceased, to be compiled in a scrapbook or photo album. Keepsakes, such as photos, clippings, and stories about the deceased, maybe a rewarding memorial later on. We also worry that we will not be able to recall the loved one well enough. We want a "slice" of the person we were in love with, something strong and true to us. One mother told me how she saved her dead daughter's hair in her jewelry box to look at and touch. Often a piece of clothing, jewelry, an item of art, a book, a piece of music, or the like, becomes a special item of remembrance.

Poetry is another meaningful way to give away at a time of loss. Sharing a poem or a song that we like or that has a special meaning for us is a lovely gesture of compassion. Poetry also seems to be referring to our deepest recesses and, like music, can have a calming effect. The only sympathy card that I remember from twenty years ago, from the hundreds that we got, included a poem that I liked, called "He's gone away." Our familiarity with, and enjoyment of, the poetry metaphor, fairy tales, and stories help us to work through our sorrow at our deepest levels.

Sharing our spiritual beliefs can also help the bereaved, particularly if we share uplifting ideas. We should express the comfort that we have gained from our convictions, but we must never attempt to force our convictions to the bereaved. Using another's misfortune to try to "sell" a specific belief system is taking unfair advantage of someone who is very weak. Each of us must choose our own values separately.

A religious or spiritual individual can be a welcoming guest to mourners. Loss and death raise many questions about the nature of life and death, why we die, and afterlife and beyond. Rabbi, minister, priest, or any other person with strong spiritual beliefs can help with some of these pressing questions. Some mourners feel so impoverished by their loss that they turn toward their former system of moral or religious belief.

From my own experience, a positive and energetic way to be with those in mourning is to meditate with them. If the bereaved are too tense or too self-conscious to meditate on themselves, the guests will meditate in a separate location, concentrating on helping the bereaved to find peace. Meditating, with mourners or separately, means sitting peacefully together to relax, clear the mind, ease, and uplift. This can be a great benefit and is also a calming and moving experience for the bereaved and tourists alike.

For a person who has never meditated before, meditation is simply sitting softly, eyes closed, intent on relaxation. There are several ways to make this relaxation happen. One of them is to watch our breathing or to concentrate on another voice, apart from ourselves. A quiet music playing in the background. Another approach is to concentrate on calming part of our whole body. Another is to count down slowly from fifty to one before we enter a state of relaxation.

We may also reflect on something other than ourselves, such as a star or a rainbow or a particular color. For each participant, group meditation can enhance the state of relaxation. For as few as two or as many individuals as there are, the participants simply sit together in a circle, on chairs, or on the floor for ten to twenty minutes of silence. The meditators might want to hold hands with each other. If so, the best way to allow the free passage of energy between the members of the community is to hold hands, each person with the right palm turned down, and the left palm turned up.

We can sit quietly with no special thought in mind, or we can have a specific emphasis as a group. It is not important for all of us to have the same focus; we could each have private thoughts or prayers. Focusing together, however, can be very moving and strong. The party will take a photo of anything it wants. Or the bereaved can be asked what should be the priority of the party. The image could be peace, or rehabilitation for the bereaved, or an easy passing of the soul of the dead. It can be a great comfort to get all one's friends together, to reflect on healing or the passing of the soul of a loved one. After the meditation, we may want to express some of our thoughts or something about our reactions or our relationship with the individual who died.

Irrespective of how we use meditation, the experience of quietly sharing together in this way can be profoundly rewarding and consoling for both the mourners and the guests. Again, because words sometimes seem so insufficient to give condolences, meditation is another way — a more powerful way — of supporting and sympathizing with grief.

Since the involvement of others is such a necessity for the deceased, it is important that this required help is not removed too quickly. It typically takes months after death for the living to cope with the loss. The bereaved need caring care all the time. If the help is withdrawn unexpectedly or without warning, it is like another loss. A friend or group of people may instead take turns checking in regularly with the bereaved in the months following the loss until he or she has recovered. If the grieving person does not seem to be healing or seems to be taking an unduly long time, it is reasonable to recommend that the grieving person consults a licensed counselor who may be of assistance.

In summary, there are many ways to help people mourn.

It's the most important thing that we do the stuff we feel comfortable doing. We should help the grieving process, not hinder it. The bereaved need to be supported at many levels, be it our participation, our energy, our sharing, our listening, our crying together, or the many practical resources that we have to give. And our simplest behavior can be of immeasurable importance.

HELPING OURSELVES WITH GRIEF: CREATIVE SURVIVAL

In order to ease our recovery from grief, we typically need a lot of support. We always take our means of help for granted before a crisis has arisen, and we are still in deep need. The three kinds of aid that aid us through depression or some other big crisis in life are self-help, environmental support (a network of people and events that brings meaning to our lives), and support for our philosophy or belief system. My goal in this chapter is to empower us to be innovative survivors and to extend our insurance support at a time when we will be in need. A well-developed support system would also increase the quality of our lives.

In a workshop, Carl and Stephanie Simonton proposed the following formula as their idea of an efficient support system:

- 25% self-support

- 20% support for the partner

- 55% support for the environment

This formula gives us a new insight to look at our lives. Few of us have a support system that is so complete. For example, the trend today is to rely heavily on the support of the partner, which definitely puts a great strain on marriages.

This can, in part, be a cause of a high rate of divorce. Likewise, our strong dependency on the help of the spouse can prevent us from developing the coping skills we need personally. If our spouse dies, we will not only suffer a massive loss of love but also lose much of our support system. Many of us do not participate any more socially than focusing on our immediate families and our jobs. We've got excuses that we don't have the time or the energy or the need for a lot more. As a result, we are depriving ourselves of much of the extensive environmental support that would benefit us.

Most of all, in times of distress, we need to be able to depend on ourselves. Self-supporting is a form of self-love. Loving oneself means soothing or strengthening oneself, listening to and acknowledging one's own emotions, paying attention to one's physical needs, and ensuring that all our needs are met rather than overlooked.

We might need to talk more or think more about it. We may need to express our feelings loudly or write our feelings in a journal. We may need work or obligation to improve our self-esteem, or we may need independence to take on less obligation. Most of all, we need to take on board our needs, regardless of what we were like before we experienced this setback.

In respecting our feelings and needs, we can demonstrate our concern for ourselves in the simple things we do to make us feel better, including taking hot baths or snorkeling every afternoon. Taking care of ourselves can mean keeping our hands occupied or physically active. Reading during times of stress or trouble can help us. Several people told me that after the loss of a loved one, they read inspirational books. On the other side, one man read books about German death camps, because that was the only agony greater for him than his own sorrow. Some people need to fly to get away from where the loss is most acutely felt. Some people need to take action, to get interested in a cause, probably a cause connected to the deceased in some way.

Often, in order to make us feel better and to let go of our sorrow, we need to take some sort of action or build a memorial for the person we loved who is gone. We also have very unique and individual needs in this field. Simply offering the deceased's belongings to someone else in need might be fulfilling enough. Some people feel the need to devote buildings or hospital rooms, or books to deceased loved ones. For others, any kind of remembrance fund is a meaningful homage to the one who's gone. My conviction is that our biggest tribute may be the manner in which we live our lives after a loss. Whatever form our tribute takes, it is vital that we honor our need for this kind of remembrance.

Another important means of reinforcement is our belief system. It is, of course, an individual matter if our values ultimately sustain us during a crisis. Our theory of life, however, has a great influence on how well we deal with pain and problems. The definitions that we assign to life, misery, and death are also the keys to how well we endure the pain and how we restructure our lives after the loss. Living a life with meaning, whatever its meaning, is better than living without moral values. For example, people who can embrace grief and crisis as part of their own growth and development find that their values are profoundly helpful in their healing and recovery.

In years gone by, seeking successful help outside of ourselves was less of a concern. We lived in the midst of extended families, where we were always surrounded by those who could be readily willing to support us with any problems. Today we live in segregated units, as individuals, as small family groups, and sometimes as single-parent families, where there are no other adults with whom to share the burden of life. Without immediate family support, we are expected to set up our own support structures. Unfortunately, many of us are not responsible for this kind of expansion. We thus have very little help in our lives and always find ourselves in dire need when trouble comes.

RECOVERY FROM GRIEF

While it may be difficult to believe, we will recover from our sorrow. Recovery from grief is restoring our freedom to live a full life and enjoy life without feelings of remorse, shame, grief, or regret. We've healed once again when we feel able to cope with our emotions and our environment, and when we can face reality and acknowledge our loss at the intestine stage, not just intellectually. Integrating our losses and reinvesting in our lives constitutes rehabilitation.

The method of healing from grief is much like the old love song to the extent that the song is finished, but the melody lingers. The depth of grief, suffering, crying, incapacitation, neediness, and all the deep feelings of mourning finally fade away. We don't forget the loved one or the suffering. However, the pain recedes. Usually, the breakdown of grief is incremental rather than immediate. In the course of healing, grief can be caused several times suddenly before completion. We could be going through various waves of pain before the waves stop coming. When we recover, the void left by the loss will still be apparent, but our reactions to it will be less extreme.

Recovery benefits from establishing recovery as an important goal and living every day as it comes, coping with both the daily routine of living and our deepest emotions. We're recovering when we can look forward to life as worth living. Complete healing means getting the prospect of remembering that one day we're going to look back and realize that we've completely grieved and endured the hardest hours of existence.

If we feel it or not, all the big changes in our lives are followed by sorrow. When we know that we've been grieving and coping before, we can see that we can heal t his time as well. It is more natural to heal and go on living than to stop in the paths of grief forever.

The low self-esteem that is typical of the mourning period also interferes with our assumption that we will recover from grief. Experience of loss momentarily undermines our self-confidence, and the mourning process depletes much of our resources. When we continue to heal, our vitality is rising, and our self-esteem typically returns. But holding on to feelings like guilt or embarrassment, or anger will hinder the restoration of our self-confidence.

Our hopes, desire, and conviction are all important to our recovery from grief. It's right to plan to recover, no matter how large the loss is. Recovery is the natural way to go. When we intend to heal, and know that it is possible, we set a target for recovery. On the other hand, if we get caught up in the common misconception that the agony of loss is never-ending, we slip into feelings of hopelessness and continued sorrow.

It is necessary to be able to recover. What is required to recover is a willingness to believe, a willingness to go on with one 's life, a willingness to let go of the pain, and a willingness to heal completely. If we can not find such willingness within ourselves, we need to investigate our resistance to healing. As described above, there are cultural obstacles to recovery from which some of our resistances stem. One common myth is that crying for a long time is a symbol of our love for the dead. The other way around, then, is that if we easily recover from sorrow, we're not really in love.

Another false assumption is that the mourners should look "poor," either physically or in terms of coping in the world. A fit, robust-looking mourner, or a mourner who is working relatively well again, is often mistrusted or misconstrued by a less conscious outsider. Perhaps the most damaging myth about mourning is that if we loved the departed, we wouldn't live our lives. There are toxic suggestions for the mourner.

The fact is, after a big tragedy, it's healthiest to take care of ourselves and repair our lives. Life is a phase of constant regeneration at all stages. Spring doesn't hesitate to come because it was followed by winter. Life comes with both good and bad experiences. However, as humans, we are expected not to be overwhelmed by either.

Negative values are another significant obstacle to healing. In order to heal, we need to believe that the complete recovery of ourselves and our lives is possible. Beliefs also become self-fulfilling prophecies, which means that we behave in the way we believe, forming our own truth. In other words, if we have seen a person who has never recovered from a loss, then we can generalize the experience and establish the impression that people do not recover from the loss of a loved one.

Thus, recovery appears to be unlikely. When we give in to such false thoughts, we end up in constant sorrow. Likewise, after a loss, we can hold on to a certain feeling, such as guilt or anger, or disappointment, that immobilizes us. People also don't accept that a feeling is going to go anywhere, and that's how they keep the feeling alive. We can hold on to those fears, such as fear of the future, and thus remain stuck in the past.

That is why it is important that we question our values and behaviors regarding healing so that our mental health and life can be recovered after the death of a loved one. Again, it's natural to heal from grief. Therefore, if we believe in healing, we will set an optimistic self-fulfilling prophecy in motion. "I'm going to heal" can become a beacon of hope on the challenging path of grief. The process of rebuilding or renewing ourselves needs all our personal strengths and resources. It's not convenient, but it's worth it. We can need to be versatile as well as able to change some of our attitudes and values. Loss can force us to re-evaluate our lives and make some changes.

Facing a loss in our lives will force a significant revision of our sense of self. We should and should take an active part in this revision. Such improvements may be important for us to restore our lives and to continue living. Recovery, then, means that you are open to further change.

Leading Yourself

Leadership must begin from the leader. I have a strong belief that what you don't have, you cannot give to someone else. So true leadership must first start from inside you before it can be projected to someone else.

Here are some important things you must do to lead

yourself effectively. **Trust your instincts**

That small voice that keeps speaking to you even in your silence. It's amazing how a lot of people fail to listen to and trust their instincts, many later regret this act. A lot of bad decisions, accidents, wrong relationships and even deaths would have been avoided if someone listened to their instinct. Learn to start trusting and following your instinct, somehow it knows what is best for you.

Believe in yourself

You must believe that you can achieve whatever you have set out to achieve. Do not rely on the impressions of others, do not give people the chance to talk you down. A lot of people give too much power to the opinions of others. Don't give approval to the wrong opinions others have about you. Believe in your abilities.

Self-talk is one very powerful tool that I recommend for anyone who wants to go far in life. Speak the kind of words you want to hear, tell yourself how good-looking you are, how important and gifted you are. You should engage in this activity at least once a day, when you wake in the morning, during the day or just before you go to bed. Tell yourself things that will elevate your mind. Your voice has a powerful impact on your mind, use it to your advantage.

Invest in self-development

Good leaders invest in the growth and development of their followers. You are the captain of your life, you are your own leader. Therefore you must invest in your growth and development. Are you desirous of achieving great things in life? If you are, you must invest more in yourself. Get relevant books, videos, audio messages and other materials that would aid you development. Make it a habit to improve yourself on a daily basis.

Take care of yourself

Man is a made off of three components, the body, the soul and the spirit. You must take good care of the three dimensions, the body by eating good food and doing regular exercises, the soul by increasing in knowledge and wisdom, and the spirit through intense religious activities. You must strive to maintain a balance in these three components to be able to lead yourself effectively.

Learn to be independent

Independence is a state of self-sufficiency, it does not imply that you will cut off from people. It means that you are not overtly dependent on anyone else for your survival. You must learn to free yourself from such relationships or habit that take away you self-sufficiency.

To lead others properly, you must first strive to lead yourself. You must be able to put your thoughts, words, action and emotions under control. The best leaders are those who have been able to lead themselves effectively. Strive daily to become a better leader of yourself and you will naturally have people follow you.

Workplace Time Management to Manage and Control Your Life

Time management is the greatest single problem that can reduce your efficiency in the workplace and disturb your life. Working people have too much to do and very less time for their personal lives and family. Most people feel besieged with responsibilities and activities, and the harder they work, the further behind they feel. This sense of being on a never-ending work can cause you to stress and fall into the reactive/responsive mode of *living.*

You repeatedly react to what is happening around you. Very soon you lose all sense of control. You feel that your life is leading you, rather than you leading your life. Regularly, you have to stand back and take stock of yourself and what you're doing. You have to evaluate your actions in the light of what is really important to you. You must manage your time rather than becoming a slave to the constant flow of actions and demands on your time. And you must organize your time to achieve balance, harmony, and inner peace.

Taking action without thoughts is the cause of every failure. Your ability to think is the most valuable trait that you have. If you are able to improve the quality of your thinking, you will be able to improve the quality of your life, sometimes immediately. Your time is precious. It is the most valuable thing. It is perishable, irreplaceable, and it can not be saved. It can only be managed by reallocated from activities of lower value to activities of higher value.

All your activities require time. And time is absolutely vital for the important relationships in your life. The very act of talking a moment to think about your time before you spend it will start to improve your personal time management immediately. Time management is not only a business tool, like a calculator or a computer. It is something that you used so that you can get more in a shorter period of time. Time management is the core skill upon which everything else in life depends.

In your work or business life, there are so many stress on your time from other people that very little of your time is yours to use as you choose. However, at home and in your personal life you can exert a marvelous amount of control over how you use your time.

How to improve self leadership

Being able to lead yourself can be a challenge for many individuals simply because they do not have the skills or experience to help themselves. Often people are left feeling that they need to be led by people of authority because they obviously have the training to do a much better job. The simple truth is that with a little self-control you have the self-leadership tools within yourself to choose whichever path that you want to travel in your life. Here are some simple techniques you can work on today so that you can do a better job of leading yourself.

Who Are You

One of the ways that many successful leaders get people motivated and working more efficiently is by getting to know the people they are leading. This is a technique you can apply to improve your self leadership skills. Take some time when you are alone *or have an hour of quiet where you can*

simply dig down and find out who you really are. Look back on past experiences and successes, and see what it took for you to achieve those goals that looked impossible at the time. Looking back you may feel a sense of accomplishment at how many major obstacles you overcame with determination and persistence. Call upon those experiences to help you lead yourself to improving your current situation.

Dream the Big Dream

Make certain that if you do not have your goals clearly laid out and written somewhere you can see them each day, that you stop and do that immediately. Not having clear goals is like shooting an arrow at a moving target from miles away. How can you possible reach your goals when you don\'t know what they are? Make your dreams and goals big, even if you have no idea how you will achieve them right now. When your goals are so big that you see all the joy they will bring you, you will find that motivation each day that will drive you right to those goals.

Reward Yourself Today

One of the problems many people have with self leadership is that they never reward themselves when they do something great. People achieve a goal and start looking towards the next project,

151

rather than taking the time to be rewarded for accomplishing that goal. When you reward yourself for reaching that level, you will be motivated to get to the next goal. These rewards do not have to be so big that you feel guilty. Simply think of ways to pamper yourself that you have been neglecting. A 30 minute massage, a new haircut, your favorite ice cream, a new magazine, and a new piece of apparel, are all ways to reward yourself and start taking better care of yourself. This is supposed to be a journey, so enjoy the entire ride.

Stop beating yourself up with each and every failure you have along the way. Failures are simply speedbumps in the road to success, and everybody has them. Self leadership is all about taking control of your mind and body, and you have to treat yourself with respect and encouragement to be motivated to get to the next step. Remember that years from now you will look back will awe and amazement at how far you came, so why not stop now and smile at how far you have come and how far you are going to go.

Qualities to work on to become a better leader

How would you describe a good leader? Some of the most important qualities for a strong leader to have are:

- Adaptability

- *Intelligence*

- *Assertiveness*

- *Conscientiousness*

- *Emotional intelligence*

The best leaders are individuals who are empowering, inspiring and positive people. They value their team and inspire them to be the best that they can be. Whether you're a manager, supervisor, or even a business owner, leading people is likely going to be a big part of your job. So, what can you do to embrace and improve these qualities in yourself and become the kind of leader that everybody wants to follow?

There are plenty of strategies that you can use to become a better leader, and the best part is that they don't take a lot of hard work; you can make small changes and implement them in your daily life straight away and start seeing positive changes in your team.

So, how do you become a better leader? Start implementing these strategies into your workday.

THE HEART OF LEADERSHIP (JOHN C. MAXWELL MODEL)

The heart of leadership is serving others first, before yourself. Here's the problem, most organizations operate from a hierarchical leadership structure. Leaders "move up" the ladder in an organization, and, once there, see themselves "above" their team. Despite its trending status – as well as its undeniable success – most people do not equate leadership to service. Rather than epitomizing humility, influence and meeting people where they are at, too many leaders think being a leader means power and authority.

Here's the good news. Some of the top performing companies like Chick-fil -A, Best Buy, UPS, Whole Foods, Starbucks, Ritz Carlton and Southwest Airlines are lead by self-described servant leaders. Their leadership qualities are people-centric, modeling servant leadership behavior and valuing service to others. They are humble – allowing their behavior to communicate their values and their appreciation for their people – and they are vigilant – in promoting the right attitude and belief systems that encourage others to succeed.

WOULD YOUR TEAM DESCRIBE YOU AS A SERVANT LEADER?

This might be a hard question to answer that might yield uncomfortable answers. But it is imperative to ask this question so you can self-correct, get the right attitude and work toward serving others using your best gifts. If your personal gain continually outweighs your desire to serve others, you are lacking the very heart of leadership – and that can be a problem – for you, your company, your family and, ultimately, your success.

John Maxwell says: "Why you lead and the way you lead are important. They define YOU, your leadership, and ultimately your contribution."

DEFINING LEADERSHIP

John C. Maxwell, 2019 Horatio Alger award winner and named the #1 leadership guru as well as author of over 75 best-selling books on leadership, sums up the definition of leadership like this, "Leadership is influence, nothing more, nothing less." So, if leadership is influence, you might be asking yourself, "How do I influence others?" Think about someone who positively influenced your life. What behavior or words were so impactful to you that you were influenced to become a better person? What about someone who negatively influenced your life? What behavior or words did they model and what effect did that have on you?

The point is that influence works two ways: positively or negatively. What matters most when it comes to influence is having a positive attitude. Really? Yes, it really is that simple. Your attitude is contagious and a positive attitude can shift the entire energy of an organization. Think about the last time someone with a negative attitude walked into the room you're in - you most likely "felt" that negative attitude without even having that person speak one word. That's why John emphasizes the importance of a positive attitude for leaders.

HOW'S YOUR ATTITUDE?

Once you've shifted your attitude, you can get to the business of being a great leader. Being a great leader is all about having a genuine willingness and a true commitment to lead others to achieve a common vision and goals through positive influence. No leader can ever achieve anything great or long-lasting all alone.

"Leadership is Influence, nothing more, nothing less." - John C. Maxwell

Just because someone has the title of leader, doesn't mean they are a leader. The greatest reflection on a leader being a true leader is whether or not they are influencing anyone. And, of course, the first place you'll see that is in the leader's people. An organization is only as great as its people. If the people aren't following, the leader isn't leading. Too often leaders get too focused on the bottom line financial results instead of growing their people and the company.

To succeed, one must stand as leaders in their organizations, regardless of position, and influence the influencers. There are several factors that can attribute to emerging as a leader. Let's take a look at the seven factors highlighted in John Maxwell's book, *The 21 Irrefutable Laws of Leadership.*

CHARACTER – WHO THEY ARE

"True leadership always begins with the inner person."

The character of a leader will filter into the entire organization and its employees. Great character will create potential for a great organization. But, it all begins with the leader's heart.

RELATIONSHIPS – WHO THEY KNOW

"Build the right kinds of relationships with the right people, and you can become the real leader in an organization."

In your sphere of influence, you must develop deep, meaningful relationships that go beyond seeing someone daily because you simply work in the same office. Relationships grow loyalty, influence and ultimately the business.

KNOWLEDGE – WHAT THEY KNOW

"Whenever I was new to an organization, I always spent a lot of time doing homework before I tried to take the lead."

New environments bring about questions to be answered. By seeking knowledge before demanding a leadership position, leaders have the chance to learn first, lead second.

INTUITION – WHAT THEY FEEL

"Leaders seek to recognize and influence intangibles such as energy, morale, timing, and momentum."

Leaders see past the obvious into realms that others cannot. This ability impacts the organization, as well as the people around them, as they can steer momentum down the best path with the most reward.

EXPERIENCE – WHERE THEY'VE BEEN

"The greater challenges you've faced as a leader in the past, the more likely followers are to give you a chance in the present."

All leaders face obstacles – in the office, at home and in their personal lives. However, through overcoming difficulties, leaders grow in great ways. By navigating through multiple tough experiences, followers will likely have more respect for where leaders have been… and where they can take the organization in the future.

PAST SUCCESS – WHAT THEY'VE DONE

"Every time I extended myself, took a risk, and succeeded, followers had another reason to trust my leadership ability – and to listen to what I had to say."

Past success doesn't guarantee future success, but it sure makes people feel more comfortable with *being led and influenced. Find ways to take on challenges and excel in them, and you'll soon be presented with new responsibilities and leadership opportunities.*

"The bottom line for followers is what a leader is capable of. They want to know whether that person can lead the team to victory."

Now, let's take a look at what is means to be a Servant Leader?

WHAT IS A SERVANT LEADER?

A servant leader's focus is on serving others rather than serving themselves or being served by others. A servant leader meets people where they are at so they can climb to the top alongside them rather than charging ahead. Maxwell wrote that his shift into a servant-leadership role happened when "[he] started to change his leadership focus to empowering others to do what [he] was doing." Servant leaders don't want to be successful all on their own. Servant leaders are looking to build a team not an empire, because they know once they build the team, success follows.

"When you decide to serve others as a leader,

the team's success becomes your success." - John C. Maxwell

He explains, "We've all encountered people in service positions with poor attitudes toward servanthood: the rude worker at the government agency, the waiter who can't be bothered with taking your order, the store clerk who talks on the phone with a friend instead of helping you.

Just as you can sense when a worker doesn't want to help people, you can easily detect whether someone has a servant's heart. When you encounter a worker who has the attitude of a servant leader, everything changes."

Mark offers you three habits that will help you become a servant leader:

1. *PERFORM SMALL ACTS OF KINDNESS.*

As leader, it's easy to get busy and forget about the people around us. When was the last time you performed small acts of kindness for others?

Start with those closest to you. Find ways today to do small things that show other people you care. You'll be blown away by the positive impact even the smallest act of kindness can have on someone.

2. *LEARN TO WALK SLOWLY THROUGH THE CROWD.*

I learned this great lesson from John Maxwell. The next time you attend a function with a number of clients, colleagues, or employees, make it your goal to connect with others by circulating among them slowly.

Focus on each person you meet. Learn names if you don't know them already. Make your agenda getting to know each person's needs, wants and desires.

Spending time with people creates not only the desire to serve them, but the connection and know-how to serve them well.

3. *MOVE INTO ACTION.*

If an attitude of servanthood is conspicuously absent from your life, the best way to change it is to start serving. Feelings will follow footsteps—if you'll begin serving with your body, your heart will eventually catch up! Then, keep at it until your heart desires to serve others well.

GETTING DOWN TO THE HEART OF IT

So, how do we get to the heart of leadership? How can we better serve others?

Maxwell offers some insight in this area in the form of some questions you can ask yourself to help with making the shift. There's eight different questions that cover the areas of adding value, every day, improvement, evaluation, the blind spot, respect, giftedness and example.

One: What can I do for people to help them succeed?

Two: What do people need from me daily that they may not want to ask for? Three: What can I work on that will help me serve people better?

Four: How will I know that I am serving people well?

Five: What is it like for the people who work with me?

Six: How can I gain value while adding value to others by serving? Seven: What do I do best that allows me to serve people better?

Eight: How can I serve people in a way that will inspire them to serve others?

After entertaining those questions, doing the appropriate research, and determining the answers that best fit what your people need from you and how you can begin to serve them, you need to put your newfound servant- leadership style into action.

"A change of heart is like gratitude. If it is unexpressed, it has little value."

- John Maxwell, bestselling author, coach and speaker

Leadership Is Influence

John Maxwell, a leadership guru, once said that "leadership is about influence. Nothing else". Maxwell may not be entirely right but he is right that influencing is a big part of leadership. Yet influencing others is one of the hardest things to do.

When my son was younger there was an incident where I was trying to get my son to eat his vegetables and was not winning the battle to get the greens into his mouth. I was just about to badger him into submission by yelling out that he would not be able to play football with me, when I recalled an important lesson on influencing. No one ever influences anyone by threats and commands. In fact, I know the No. 1 rule of influencing someone (especially your children) is to make the vegetables more appealing — but how? I decided to showcase to him that everyone else was eating them and enjoying it tremendously.

So, I just told my son that all his friends were eating their vegetables and he would be the only one not doing so. He somehow seemed happy to chomp on his greens. People love to follow the crowd. No matter how much you believe that you are not influenced by others, the truth is we are influenced by what others are doing and saying.

We tend to enjoy songs that others listen to – the

best example being the Gangnam Style. We tend to dress like others. We are influenced all the time by all sorts of people and fads. This happen so often, we even tend to engage in unlawful acts when we see others do it.

A few years ago, the crime rate in a town started to rise. There were warnings and threats issued and strict laws enacted. There were big "Do Not Steal" posters but these didn't reduce the crime rate. In fact, crime became worse in those areas where warnings were posted. Finally, there was a smart campaign that highlighted that the majority of people did not steal.

Surprisingly, the campaign worked. In London, a new campaign kicked off called the "99 percent". The campaign had posters all over London stating that "99 percent of young Londoners DO NOT COMMIT serious violence". And guess what happened? People were influence by these posters and crime started to decline.

Influence is critical for our success in life and in business. So, how do you influence?

There are numerous parts to influencing effectively. According to research done in Harvard by Nalini Ambady, it takes only six seconds for people to judge us. Ambady provided university students six seconds worth of footage (with no audio) of professors teaching and asked these students to rate the teachers. She kept the ratings and at the end of the semester, compared the six second ratings to the ratings from students who actually attend the full semester of classes of these professors.

She found that even with six seconds, the students evaluations of the professors were amazingly similar (and accurate) to the ratings of students who underwent a full semester of classes. These six seconds are our window of influence. Body language, words, your appearance, harnessing the power of story-telling and using various means of concessions are all part of the influencing arsenal.

What is influence?

At Leaderonomics, we define "Influence as the ability to move others into action." Whenever we can change someone's thought process and convince them to pursue a course of action, we have exercised influence, hence demonstrated leadership. The heart of strategic influencing is to gain willing cooperation instead of mere compliance.

It's about getting others to follow us because they want to and not because they have to. Influencing moves work from being merely transactional to relational. The most effective way to influence *others is first to build a relationship of trust.*

On Sept 18, 1978, in Jonestown Guyana, 909 followers of the People's Temple, led by cult-leader Jim Jones, died by cyanide poisoning in what is called the largest mass-suicide in modern history. How did Jones come to command such enormous influence over his followers' thoughts and actions? How did over 700 adults willingly feed themselves and 200 of their children with poison at the request of their leader? Social psychologists identified the ability to build relational trust as a key factor for cult-leaders' massive influence.

Jones was often described by his followers as someone who was loving and was deeply concerned about his followers' well-being amidst his domineering and controlling personality. They loved him and trusted him completely. Here lies the powerful truth about influence: The level of influence you have on others is directly proportionate to the level of trust they have in you. And trust does not happen automatically. It is something you need to work on.

Influencing secrets

There are a number of other "secrets" to enable you to become better at influencing. Alex Pentland, a professor at MIT, conducted an experiment where he attached digital recording devices to business leaders to monitor their speech and body language over the course of a social dinner. A week later, he was able to predict with 87% accuracy how these leaders would fare in a business presentation which was rated by judges. He did this without listening to a word of the presentation. How did he do it?

A key part to influencing others, especially judges or interviewers, is not what you say but how you portray yourself. Are you confident, passionate, single-minded and committed to the cause you are presenting? The delivery of your message may be much more important than what is said.

Smile more?

Surprisingly, many believe that smiling more helps you to influence better as you come across as warm and personable. Research, though, shows that smiling makes no difference to your ability to better influence (although the strength of a person's smile has a positive effect on customer satisfaction in the service industry). Neither does body posture. Nor hand movement. So, what are factors that make a difference?

The most important body part for influencing is your eye. Research from the University of Toronto stipulates that "eye contact is magnetic." Eye contact with each other signals attraction and creates a link that pulls people together. So, while trust may take time to build, having eye contact with people you interact with at work and socially is something that can be easily done.

Final thoughts

All of us are influencing people or are being influenced in some way or form every day of our lives. Building trust gives you the seed of influence. But more than that, your body language plays a big part in how people view and judge you. Learn to use your eye contact and learn to include stories into your presentations and discussions.

Everyone needs to influence every day. Learning to influence will only help you to become a better leader.

Understand Your Own Leadership Style

In order to become a better leader, understanding your current leadership style is the first crucial step. Ask yourself:

- What are your strengths?

- What are your weaknesses?

- Which areas need improvement the most?

- What are your major leadership characteristics?

- Do these qualities help or hinder your leadership?

Be as honest with yourself as you can, even if the answers aren't exactly what you wanted to hear about yourself. If you're struggling to determine your leadership style, it might be worth asking some members of your team to be honest with you; explain to them that you are trying to improve yourself as a leader and want their honest feedback on what you do well and what you could improve on.

Once you have determined which areas need some work, you will be able to get some direction when it comes to the best ways to start improving your leadership qualities.

Be a Good Role Model

Transformational leaders aren't just inspiring individuals; they are impeccable role models for their team. A good leader doesn't just talk; they walk the walk too. They exemplify the characteristics and behaviors that they want to see from their team. And as a result, their team members admire them as a leader and want to emulate those behaviors.

Research suggests that successful leaders are able to foster specific beliefs and use them to inspire their team. As a result, teams are more optimistic and tend to have higher standards for both achievement and performance.

If you want to become a better leader, work on displaying the qualities that you would like to see in your team.

Be Passionate About What You Do

It's unlikely that you would look to somebody for leadership and guidance if they didn't seem bothered about the goals of the group. A great leader is not only focused on getting tasks finished; they have a genuine enthusiasm and passion for their work, and it shows.

Work on developing this leadership quality by thinking of different ways that you can show your passion for what you do and share it with your team. Make sure that your team members know that you are genuinely proud of their accomplishments and progress; when a team member shares an idea with the rest of the group, make sure that you let them know just how much you appreciate their contribution.

Encourage Creativity

Transformational leadership is defined by intellectual stimulation. Leaders who are highly focused on just getting tasks done, rather than allowing and actively encouraging team members to express their ideas and creativity, do not tend to be the most transformational.

In order to be an effective leader, you should:

• *Offer new challenges*

• *Provide ample support to team members in order to help them achieve these goals*

• *Make sure that the goals are within the grasp of team members' abilities*

• *Encourage people to stretch their limits*

Improve Your Listening and Communication Skills

A focus on providing effective one-to-one communication with team members is another highly important quality of good leadership. Transformational, inspiring leadership is at its most effective when leaders are able to clearly communicate their vision to their team members, who are then inspired and motivated by it.

A good leader should:

• *Express sincere care and concern for team members both verbally and nonverbally*

• *Keep the lines of communication open and encourage clear communication between team member and themselves and within the team*

• *Ensure that team members feel that they are able to make contributions*

• *Provide recognition to team members for*

their achievements Be a Positive Person

The best leaders are characterized by their genuinely optimistic, upbeat attitude that becomes a source of inspiration for others. When the leader appears to be apathetic or discouraged, members of the team are more likely to follow suit.

As a leader, even when things aren't looking too great and your team begins to feel disheartened, it's important to try and stay positive. While this doesn't mean always looking at everything through rose-tinted glasses and forcing false positivity, it does mean maintaining a sense of optimism
— trying to see the bright side to situations and having hope even in the face of a challenge.

Encourage Your Team to Make Contributions

As a leader, make sure that your team members know that you welcome and value their ideas, suggestions and contributions. A democratic or participative leader is somebody who encourages active involvement from their team, rather than simply telling people what to do. Although they may have the final say over decisions, they encourage their team to share their visions, ideas, plans and changes in a project.

Research has shown that when leaders have a democratic or participative leadership style, it leads to several benefits for the entire team, including:

• *Better productivity*

• *More loyalty amongst employees*

• *A better workplace environment*

• *Stronger team relationships and better teamwork*

• *More creative problem-solving*

• *Greater*

commitment to the

task at hand **Be a**

Motivator

The best leaders don't just tell their team what they need to be doing; they provide inspirational motivation to encourage them to do it. As you probably know, being inspirational isn't always the easiest of tasks, but the good news is that you don't need to give lengthy motivational speeches every day.

To be an inspirational leader, work on becoming:

• *Genuinely passionate about the ideas you're heading or the goals you're working towards with your team*

• *Getting team members involved and included in the process*

• *Valuing contributions*

• *Offering recognition and praise for the accomplishments of individuals and your team as a whole*

Another hugely important quality of any good leader is that they know offering effective rewards and recognition is one of the best ways to make sure that their team feels appreciated and valued, which leads to greater happiness and satisfaction at work.

It probably comes as no surprise that people who're satisfied in their job tend to perform better at work. And as a leader, offering rewards and recognition doesn't have to be something that takes up a lot of effort or money. It can include:

• *Genuinely saying thank you to team members who have contributed their ideas and suggestions*

• *Praising the team for achieving their goals*

• *Offering team or individual incentives when working towards goals and following through with them*

Be Willing to Learn from Your Team

Leadership is by no means a one-way street, and the best leaders know that they aren't just teachers or coaches; there's also a lot they can learn from their

175

team members.

The best leaders are humble and accept that there's no way they can know
everything; even if they have the best qualifications or the most experience compared to their team members, there's always going to be something that somebody else can teach them, and they are open to learning as much as possible. A good leader is never too proud to admit that they didn't know something, and thank somebody for showing them.

Ask for Feedback

The main quality that separates the good leaders from the rest is the fact that they aren't improving their leadership qualities for themselves; they are doing it because they know that it will have a good impact on their team.

Regularly ask your team for feedback on your leadership performance; after all, they are the people that you are leading and will be able to provide you with details about what you can do to improve your leadership skills and qualities in your individual situation. Sitting down with your team members and asking for honest feedback, then taking what they say into account and working on those areas, is the best way to make sure that you are the kind of leader that your team looks up to and is inspired by. And along with getting valuable feedback that you can use, you'll also make sure that your team members know their opinions and ideas are valued.

Self help to leadership basically focuses on creating personal leadership skills such that in any endeavor, they take command, stand for ideals, guide others and make strong decisions. This challenging skill separates them from others, and the greatest leaders were not born leaders, they became over a phase of time by slowly toughening up to criticism, resolving opposition and grew in strength by learning to rise, by standing firmly even in most difficult situations. However, people who desire to be leaders or who are keen to nurture leadership qualities can strengthen their skills and encourage to promote their aims.

Self help to leadership is a ladder to accomplish power that is expected to be started in the early stages of life so that a person is capable to taking responsibility. It is a must that anything started should be completed and any work done should be the best. This thought prepares even young children to gain incredible satisfaction on getting things done right. Self help to leadership can be initiated with young people joining clubs and student councils, while adults can get enrolled with some community club or church or some other business networking group. Initially, occupying a low power position and later gaining experience to responsible positions is the right entry level for aspirant leaders.

Volunteering work such as providing assistance to people in need, fund raising, performing specific services, etc teaches being and handling the authority role of leadership. Volunteers normally have less pressure and it is the best to understand self help to leadership. Initiate and take up new challenges with confidence as holding a leadership position in a small team gives an opportunity to widen to new ability levels, organize and study problems and to take a responsible part. Being responsible is one of the focused self help to leadership that allows you to concentrate and complete.

Self help to leadership is a ladder to claim power, but this needs honing speaking skills, writing and presentation style as well. These are the valuable skills that offer a realistic evaluation of leadership style and maintaining calm, even if there is lot of turmoil going inside, is one of the unbeatable talents that need to be honed. Self help to leadership need not necessarily begin from a working place or associations; it can slowly start with your group of friends as well. Look for a right opportunity and kindle a special interest or even a common interest and keep making agendas, minutes, update regularly, make simple alterations, offer ideas and guidelines, and slowly this will become *professional.*

Staying active most of the times is a great quality and develop a good listening skill, besides reading extensively about leaders, business magnets, politicians and many more famous people will give you guidance and inspiration. Unknowingly, you will realize that all excellent leaders of yester years as well have faced typical problems of yours, but knowing their style of handling the situations will be of great help.

Meet people from different backgrounds as it boosts your confidence level and offers valuable experience. Observing and studying others and handling adverse reactions without any harsh expression on the face are certain qualities that is tough to be developed, but is essential as self help to leadership.

A Leader Must Conquer Self

In far too many instances, our greatest and most dangerous enemy is our self. Sometimes this is because of attitude, sometimes because of an inability to introspectively examine our strengths and weaknesses, and at still other times it is a result of our behavior and/or reaction to a variety of circumstances. Plato stated this perfectly, "The first and greatest victory is to conquer yourself; to be conquered by yourself is of all things most shameful and vile." When it comes to one's ability to be a truly effective leader, this is even more relevant. True leaders must understand and honestly appraise their strengths and weaknesses, and adapt as necessary to become better and more effective.

1. When one considers a position of leadership, he should first examine his reasons for doing so. What are his true motives? Does he want to lead because he feels he can make a real difference, or because he desires the recognition and/ or accolades? Will the individual commit to the time and effort? Will this potential leader know himself so well that he can overcome adversity and obstacles, rather be saddled an incapacitated by them? When one is in a leadership position, there can be no place for self doubt. A true leader has undergone training and learned and applied techniques and philosophies of leadership. Although I have trained over a thousand potential leaders over more than three decades, only those who first commit to self understanding and take from that true inner strength, have ended up being able to fulfill the position in an effective and consistent manner.

2. Many people claim to know themselves, but few actually take the time to do a thorough self examination. I have observed that while most of those in leadership present themselves publicly as confident, in reality most are not nearly that self assured. Many of those leaders

who some believe to be driven by their egos, are not egoistic at all, but rather so insecure that they portray themselves that way to cover up their insecurities. When someone understands themselves fully, it gives them the opportunity to learn more, understand more, make wiser decisions, use better judgment, and overall demonstrate far greater wisdom, than those unwilling or unable to undergo this essential exercise. Self understanding is an essential, yet often overlooked part of leadership training. Since no two individuals are alike in every way, there can be no thorough and complete leadership training without an emphasis on customizing training to an individual and his needs.

Once someone conquers himself, there is very little he cannot overcome. Self understanding provides a leader with the strength and courage to face difficult circumstances and challenges, and thus turn adversity into victory.

CPSIA information can be obtained
at www.ICGtesting.com
Printed in the USA
BVHW032050030321
601492BV00010B/536

9 781801 572231